To:
Wayne —
Please give
you at Jake's.
All the best to
you and family.
Hope you make it
our way some day
soon!

Mike D___

SEND ME:
A SOLDIER'S STORY

The Story of Chief Warrant Officer Three Mike Dean USA (RET), Former Member of the Unit—America's Most Secret Special Operations Team

MIKE DEAN

FOREWORDS BY
TONEY MICHAEL BUCCHI VADM USN (RET)
AND
GEORGE HILL, INDIANA PACERS

iUniverse LLC
Bloomington

SEND ME: A SOLDIER'S STORY
THE STORY OF CHIEF WARRANT OFFICER THREE MIKE DEAN USA (RET), FORMER MEMBER OF THE UNIT—AMERICA'S MOST SECRET SPECIAL OPERATIONS TEAM

Copyright © 2013 Mike Dean.

All rights reserved. No part of this book may be used or reproduced by any means, graphic, electronic, or mechanical, including photocopying, recording, taping or by any information storage retrieval system without the written permission of the publisher except in the case of brief quotations embodied in critical articles and reviews.

While the stories portrayed in this work are based upon real events and real people, the names were changed for security purposes. Additionally, codes names mentioned have been previously published or declassified by the U.S. Government.

Send Me—A Soldier's Story has undergone the review process by the Department of Defense: Office of Security Review. While they are not endorsing this book, or the accuracy of the material, they have cleared the book for open publication in accordance with the compliance of the author to amend certain material.

The views presented are those of the author and do not necessarily represent the views of Department of Defense or its Components.

The cover photo as well as the photos appearing in this book are personal photos either taken by, or belonging to, Michael J. Dean.

Unless otherwise indicated, all Scripture quotations are taken from the New King James Version of the Bible. Copyright ©1982 by Thomas Nelson, Inc. Used by permission. All rights reserved. (Emphasis in scripture added by the author.)

iUniverse books may be ordered through booksellers or by contacting:

iUniverse LLC
1663 Liberty Drive
Bloomington, IN 47403
www.iuniverse.com
1-800-Authors (1-800-288-4677)

Because of the dynamic nature of the Internet, any web addresses or links contained in this book may have changed since publication and may no longer be valid. The views expressed in this work are solely those of the author and do not necessarily reflect the views of the publisher, and the publisher hereby disclaims any responsibility for them.

Any people depicted in stock imagery provided by Thinkstock are models, and such images are being used for illustrative purposes only.

Certain stock imagery © Thinkstock.

ISBN: 978-1-4917-0682-4 (sc)
ISBN: 978-1-4917-0683-1 (hc)
ISBN: 978-1-4917-0707-4 (e)

Library of Congress Control Number: 2013916007

Printed in the United States of America.

iUniverse rev. date: 11/19/2013

In Memory of

Col. James Raymond "Trooper" Tirey, USA (RET)

Jim was a dedicated soldier who served this
country in ways we will never know.

To Wish for Our Heroes Foundation

To the Wounded Warriors, and to all the men and women in uniform
who have served, are now serving, and to those who will serve.

The defense of this country rests upon the shoulders of your sacrifice.

CONTENTS

Acknowledgements ix
Author's Note xi
Glossary xiii
Prologue xv
Foreword by Toney Michael Bucchi VADM USN (RET) xvii
Foreword by George Hill, Indiana Pacers xix
Introduction xxi

Chapter 1   Washington D.C. 1
Chapter 2   Crimes of War 9
Chapter 3   Skyhawk 27
Chapter 4   Gangway 33
Chapter 5   Port Calls 45
Chapter 6   A Time of Transition 55
Chapter 7   Desert Shield / Desert Storm 65
Chapter 8   Honduras 79
Chapter 9   15th MI 85
Chapter 10   Full Circle 95

Epilogue: A History of Success through Perseverance 103
Appendix: Wish for Our Heroes Foundation 115
About the Author 119
Endnotes 121

Special thanks and acknowledgment to:

Jesus, my Savior

My wife Susie: We have come full circle.

My parents: Thomas and Beverly

My brother Steve

My children: Angela, Lily, Earl, stepdaughter Alexis, stepson Chance, and my grandchildren

My friends: You know who you are.

Nick A. Santini SGM USA (Ret) (selected and hired by Harry G. Riley and Col. Jerry King): for a lifetime of dedication and support of the Unit

Clay Greagor: owner of Last Flight Out, Key West, Florida. You made me realize this book was possible.

In Clay's Words: "First you must dare to dream . . . about who you want to be, where you'd like to go, and what you would like to do. Then you must think positive . . . get that state of mind to help you through your journey. Lastly, you must have the courage to pursue your goals . . ." (Excerpted from *Last Flight Out,* by Clay Greagor)

AUTHOR'S NOTE

The stories portrayed in this work are based upon real events and real people; names were changed for the protection of those who served.

GLOSSARY

AO—Area of Operations

CJA—[The] Center for Justice and Accountability

CW3—Chief Warrant Officer Three

DI—Drill Instructor

FBO—Fixed Base Operator

Green Beret—Highly trained branch of the United States Army, specializing in unconventional or guerrilla warfare. In 1987 those Special Forces personnel not deactivated after the Vietnam War (1959-1975) were incorporated into the U.S. Special Operations Command

ICTY—International Criminal Tribunal for the Former Yugoslavia

IO—Indiana Ocean

JOC—Joint Operations Center

MCRD—Marine Corps Recruit Depot

Med—Mediterranean

NATO—North Atlantic Treaty Organization

Ops—Short for operations

SAS—Special Air Service; Britain's tier-one special operations commando unit

SH-3 Helicopter—Sikorsky SH-3 Sea King: twin-engine anti-submarine warfare helicopter

Spook—a term used to describe espionage agents or spies

SWO—Senior Warrant Officer

UCMJ—Uniform Code of Military Justice

WOCS—Warrant Officer Candidate School

PROLOGUE

Veritas Omnia Vincula Vincit
"Truth Conquers All Chains"

Colonel Jerry King, founder of the Unit, designed its crest with the bold statement "Send Me." The unit's motto is "Truth Conquers All Chains," and its crest depicts an eagle grasping a claymore—the traditional broadsword used by the medieval Scottish highlanders to repel the English invaders—and wrapped in a metal chain.

The crest came about because of a number of leading members of the unit, including Colonel King, had Scottish ancestry. The outer frame of the crest was in the form of a leather belt normally worn around a kilt. One of the nine links in the chain was broken as a reminder of the failed

Eagle Claw mission (Desert One). Each of the eight other complete links represented one of the eight men who died at Desert One.

The words "Send Me" were inscribed on the blade of the claymore. It is a quotation from the Bible, Isaiah 6:8: "Also I heard the voice of the Lord, saying, 'Whom shall I send, and who will go for Us?' Then I said, 'Here am I! Send me.'"[1]

FOREWORD

Mike Dean has done a masterful job of blending stories from a unique military career path with colorful details of his journey, while weaving in accurate historical events. Throughout this "Soldier's Story," he never loses sight of a higher calling and the impact each of our life's stories can have on family, friends and associates.

As a military career man myself with over 33 years in the U.S. Navy, I found Mike's styles of writing intriguing, which generated many personal memories of my own life's encounters.

Well done to Mike Dean! The treasures captured within the pages of this book will certainly live on well past his own days, and I am sure, will impact the lives of his descendants, and others like me.

Toney Michael Bucchi VADM USN (Ret)

FOREWORD

My job as a basketball player is simple: help my team win basketball games. Our military members place their lives on the line each and every day, so that we can all live our lives without fear of those who would like to cause us harm. Born and raised in Indiana, I feel like we have an obligation to do everything in our power to assist our Hoosier military members. I have spent time at Indiana military bases with Wish for Our Heroes, and I've seen the struggles our military members face first-hand. I believe in what Wish for Our Heroes is doing to help address the everyday needs of our Hoosier Heroes, and I encourage other Hoosiers to step forward and join the effort.

Mike Dean has deep Indiana roots, and through the chronicle of his military service, he also hopes to assist as many military members as possible. Let's all join Mike in working together to support our Heroes!

George Hill, Indiana Pacers

INTRODUCTION

I was born into a military family in a small Midwest town called Beech Grove, just a short distance south of Indianapolis, Indiana. The town I grew up in was exactly how one might picture a small Midwest town. We enjoyed the peacefulness of Sunday afternoons after spending the morning in church. We had the classic Indiana scenery of cornfields on the outskirts of town and the two-story brick buildings along Main Street. And as is common in so many small towns, we had the proverbial downtown restaurant where the older men gathered early in the morning to drink coffee and complain about politics and grain prices as they reminisced about the "good old days."

Some would argue that small towns are boring. For me, growing up in Beech Grove created the best childhood memories. When I was a child, there was nothing better than having the run of the town during the summer months. Everywhere I looked I saw familiar faces. When I was hot and thirsty, I simply stopped playing and took a drink from a neighbor's garden hose. During the school year I played with the neighborhood kids all afternoon until Mom called me in for supper. Our town also had the Norman Rockwell picturesque soda fountain at the downtown drugstore my grandpa used to take me to—complete with a white-capped attendant behind the counter.

Anyone who has grown up in such a wonderful environment can also envision the school I attended. Every parent knew the teachers from church and said hello to them in the grocery store. Our principal was a surrogate father to many young boys—a disciplinarian, but kindhearted underneath. Unfortunately for me, I viewed school as a necessary evil. Compulsory education did not satisfy the longing I had to be out in the real world. As other students studied to get better grades on their exams, I stared out the window dreaming of faraway places. Little did I know that someday I would travel the world, experiencing many of those things I had only daydreamed about as an adolescent.

Being young and impulsive, and not understanding the value of an education, I dropped out of high school to join the U.S. Marine Corps. The military seemed like a fitting door for me to step through since I had grown up in a military family. My father had been a marine, and later my brother would serve in the U.S. Air Force. Donning a military uniform came naturally to me, and the professionals in the Marine Corps quickly taught me the discipline which most eighteen-year-olds need. Along with military discipline came the epiphany of what I must do to be successful. Deeply regretting dropping out of school, I no longer viewed education as a burden. As a matter of fact, furthering my education became one of my greatest goals in life.

After completing my GED I went on to pursue postsecondary education. While in the service I earned my associate degree from Mohegan Community College, a bachelor's degree in business from the University of Central Texas, and a master's certificate in government contracting from George Washington University. As my military career progressed I obtained a pilot's license, an FAA airframe and power plant license, became an open water certified scuba diver, and completed a host of other military schools and Special Operations training courses.

Altogether my career has spanned three branches of the military. I began my service in the Marine Corps, made an intra-service move to the Navy, and then again to the Army. It was during my service in the

Army that I was tapped to become part of the Unit. I'm also proud to say the military tradition has continued in my family. My son served in the Coast Guard, my son-in-law serves in the Air Force, my daughter serves in the Army, and my stepson serves in the Navy.

I'm now retired from the Army, but I still work as a civilian with the Department of the Defense. I've logged over thirty-three years of military and civil service with citations and awards including the Bronze Star from Operation Desert Shield/Desert Storm, and the Legion of Merit at retirement. In the course of my life I also taught Principles of Management for Central Texas College in Honduras, owned three small businesses, served as the Industrial Advisory Board Chair for the Consortium for Embedded Systems—National Science Foundation, graduated from the Defense Acquisition University Level Three, and currently I'm active in my local church and community.

As I consider my life thus far, I'm astonished at how many things have come full circle. I left a small town in Indiana, and now I reside once again in a small community in Indiana. I married my high school sweetheart when I was young. We had a daughter together when my wife was seventeen, only a short while after her father passed away. Being young and immature, we ended up divorced amidst the stress. Many years later we reunited, remarried, and God has blessed us with great happiness. With my wife by my side, a beautiful country home on ten acres with woods and a small lake, and our rescued chocolate lab named Roxie, who could ask for anything more? As a line from a well-known country song asks, "Who says you can't come back?"

This book has been in my heart for more than five years. It is a confluence of the value of the memories of my grandparents; the summers I spent visiting relatives while helping them on their Michigan farm; my awareness of the challenges the older generation faced during the Great Depression; and the thought of how wonderful it would've been to have their stories recorded. As I document my experiences, I consider the picture of Abraham Lincoln hanging behind my desk. It triggers thoughts of my great-aunt who was 100 years old in 1963. It's hard to believe I knew someone who was born only two years before Lincoln's assassination. My portrait of him shows the word "Perseverance" at the top and lists many of his failures at the bottom. It was through perseverance that he became the sixteenth President of the United States, and his resolve exemplifies my admiration for the previous generation—of how they overcame hardships with grit and determination.

Life is replete with axioms; one of the most universal is that we will all experience trials and tribulations. Though they are unavoidable, we're told in Scripture to "glory in tribulations, knowing that tribulation produces perseverance." I've discovered that many of my greatest accomplishments have come after—or as a result of—a failure or hardship. It's those experiences, and the attitude of not giving up, that have carried me through. So in faith I decided to begin recording my memories as I want my children and grandchildren to have knowledge of my experiences. It's also my desire, if possible, to inspire those who read my story. I want others to know that whatever they dream, wherever they journey, if they believe in themselves and persevere—even when doors might appear to be closed—if they trust the Lord, He will guide their every step.

I say with great passion that I'm proud to be one of America's sons. To me, serving our country in the Armed Forces means more than just buttoning up a uniform. To paraphrase one of America's greatest generals, military service is about duty, honor, and country. Having grown up in a military family, having served our nation in uniform, and having served alongside America's bravest men and women, I have the highest regard for all who serve in the United States Armed

Forces—especially those who have given the ultimate sacrifice. That's why I've chosen to donate all the proceeds from this book to the Wish for Our Heroes Foundation.

Every soldier's story is unique. This one is mine. What I offer you is the story of a young marine who, after transferring to the U.S. Navy, served aboard the USS John F. Kennedy, later in the Army as a young warrant officer who faced the challenges of Operation Desert Shield/Desert Storm, and afterward served in Military Intelligence finding himself knee-deep within the Unit.

Needless to say, the Lord has allowed me to fly a long way from a small town south of Indianapolis. My hope is that you will enjoy taking this journey with me. Now sit back, relax, and enjoy the flight.

1
WASHINGTON D.C.

Washington D.C.'s Dulles airport is always hectic. I was thankful to exit the busy terminal at 5:10 PM to board flight number 1105 to Milan, Italy. As I entered the airplane, I stepped into the aisle toward my window seat just behind the exit row. Directly ahead of me was an attractive woman who was also getting settled for the long flight. I hoped I would be seated next to her. However, the fate of pleasant company was not on my side.

The man I wound up being seated with was at least six feet four inches tall, and he must have weighed around two hundred and seventy pounds. Not only was he fully occupying his entire seat, he was also spilling over into mine. Flying across the Atlantic is wearisome by itself, but having my personal space invaded certainly wasn't a forecast of what I would consider a pleasant way to fly. As I took my seat, I quickly scanned the appearance of my husky neighbor. He was a middle-aged man with jet black hair, brown eyes, square jaw, and he wore a tailor-made black pinstriped business suit with a crisp white shirt and no tie. He struggled maneuvering his large frame as he placed a black briefcase under the seat in front of him. I glanced at the briefcase spotting the initials "SLS."

As the passengers continued to situate themselves, the flight attendant handed my oversized traveling companion a cup of coffee. My olfactory senses were attacked as the coffee aroma floated toward me blended with his Polo cologne. Peripherally I could see the cup of coffee disappearing inside his sausage-like fingers only revealing a wisp of steam rising up. As I turned fully to my right, I caught the eyes of the woman across the aisle, the same woman with whom I'd hoped to be seated. I couldn't help noticing how attractive she was with her short blonde hair, green eyes, long slender legs, and high heels. Most men would've been compelled to take a second glance. As I did, I was intrigued by a noticeable look of *déjà vu* in her eyes. It appeared as though she was evaluating whether she had seen me somewhere before. This wasn't just fanciful chauvinistic thinking. I could tell she was clicking through previous contacts in her mind.

I continued to make mental notes of what was going on around me as we began to taxi to the runway. I also thought of Steve Pelley who had been in place over thirty days. A rotation was normally thirty to forty-five days. Like most operations, this one had gone on for some time. At the moment I didn't realize how our efforts to hunt down, snatch, and indict war criminals from the Bosnian Serb conflict would end up lasting so long. In this particular operation my job was to "deconflict" intelligence operations at a Joint NATO Center about two hours from Milan, Italy.

As our flight began climbing over the Atlantic, I thought about the reason my unit was involved in operations in Eastern Europe. From 1992 to 1995, the people of Bosnia had endured a wave of ethnic violence as Serbian and Bosnian Serb armed forces launched a campaign of terror against Bosnia's Muslim population. Their war against civilians shocked the global conscience while adding the term "ethnic cleansing" to the world's lexicon of atrocities.[2]

By 1992, reports of war crimes spurred the United Nations Security Council to take action. In May of 1993 the UN created the International Criminal Tribunal for the former Yugoslavia (ICTY)—the first international war crimes tribunal since World War II. At the same time the UN Security Council established so-called "safe areas" in Bosnia-Herzegovina with the mission of protecting the civilian population. However, indefinite rules of engagement and limited resources hampered the UN peacekeepers.[3] On July 11, 1995, UN forces effectively surrendered Srebrenica, a "safe area to be protected by all means," to advancing Bosnian Serb forces. Led by General Ratko Mladic, Bosnian Serb forces committed the largest mass murder in Europe since the Holocaust: At least 8,000 Bosnian Muslim men and boys were massacred while thousands of women were subjected to mass rape and forced deportation.[4] The ICTY officially declared that the Srebrenica Massacre constituted an act of genocide.[5]

As our current operations were underway in Eastern Europe, the Unit was under a joint review. There were those within the U.S. Congress, and within the upper echelon of the military, who were not fond of anonymous intelligence gathering units or their missions. But, because of the Unit's status and effectiveness within the special operations community, and in conjunction with the protection of the Assistant Secretary of Defense for Special Operations, our operations were still very much alive even after several attempts to rein them in. Intelligence gathered from sources, along with electronic surveillance, was critical in the evaluation of potential options for capturing those identified as war criminals from the Bosnian Serb conflict—those whom the ICTY wanted taken into custody.[6]

About four hours into the ten-hour flight, my mind and body were jolted back into the misfortune of my cramped surroundings. I was unwillingly being subjected to the commotion of Sausage Fingers with a mixed drink in one hand, and with his other hand motioning to a man behind him—an older balding gentleman with thick eyebrows and glasses. Both of them spoke German. I couldn't help noticing how the attractive woman across the aisle had suddenly perked up and hung onto every word they were saying. I peered out the window into the dark of night wondering if this was casual conversation or something else. In my line of work you were programmed to listen, observe, and analyze. I sometimes felt like a Pavlovian experiment: The bell rings and I begin salivating for the next bit of information.

About halfway through the flight, and after dinner was over, the lights in the passenger section were dimmed. Having very little rest from the night before, I pulled my window shade down and began to drift off to sleep. I hoped Sausage Fingers wouldn't jab me with his elbow or spill his drink in my lap so I could get a decent nap. As my mind began to fade into another world, I was thinking back to the day I began this peculiar but exciting journey.

As I looked out the window of the airplane on my way to Marine boot camp in San Diego, I couldn't help thinking about my father's reaction during my departure. After stopping by my grandparents' house to say goodbye, my parents drove me to the airport in Indianapolis. As the time approached for me to leave, the actuality of where I was heading began to sink in. Dad began to sob as I said my final goodbyes. He was a "man's man." It was unusual for me to see him cry. The truth is, we were both getting emotional.

"Don't cry, Dad. It's okay," I consoled him as we hugged each other.

At the time I didn't understand why he was getting so choked up. Later in my life, when I would see my own son off to military service, I would understand more fully why my father had been so emotional. From a father's perspective you realize how quickly time goes by. You begin to reflect on the time you've spent with your son, wishing you had a little more. As I hugged my father that day, I thought of a Bible verse in James 4:14 which tells us: "For what is your life? It is even a vapor that appears for a little time and then vanishes away."

Dad, having been in my shoes, also understood how I would leave that day as a child, but would return as a man. Of course, like most eighteen-year-olds I felt indestructible. My parents on the other hand were fully aware I was entering a world of weapons, violence, and the ubiquitous possibility of losing my life. Even a fleeting thought of losing a son or daughter in conflict is difficult for any parent to deal with. For me, there was no turning back. My next stop was the U.S. Marine Corps Recruit Depot in San Diego, California.

I was a high school dropout, married and with a daughter. It hadn't take long for me to realize how dropping out of school wasn't the wisest choice I'd ever made. I knew I couldn't properly provide for a family while working minimum wage jobs. I was heading down a dead-end road. I had to change my course and move in a direction with a future. I could have signed on the dotted line to enter any branch of the service, but I chose the Marines, maybe because dad had been a Marine.

Admittedly, I had some romantic notions about military service, probably due to all the old war movies my grandfather and I watched together when I was a child. When you're young you can almost picture yourself right in the middle of the battles. Like many children of the Vietnam era, I grew up playing Army with the neighborhood boys. We shot our air guns at an imaginary enemy, threw dirt clod hand grenades while taking possession of enemy territory created in our minds, and hid in the bushes from enemy vehicles passing by on the streets in front of our houses. As it is with most things in life, reality is not in partnership with the romantic pictures painted by our minds.

Like most young men, I had no idea what was waiting for me at boot camp. I'd heard the stories of the tough-as-nails drill instructors and the rigorous training, but a person really has no idea until they experience it for themselves. I was nervous, but I was determined to succeed. My lack of achievement thus far helped me realize how I would never be satisfied with a lackadaisical approach to life. I dreamed big and needed the stimulative affects of activity and progress.

After a long flight, I exited the plane and was immediately ushered onto a bus with the other marine recruits. The bus ride was short. The MCRD was located right off the runway of the San Diego airport. I had also heard stories of the Marine Corps drill instructor's proficient and prolific use of expletives, but it was surrealistic to experience it firsthand. Now they were in my face—literally. They were mean and loud. It was almost superhuman how they noticed every single movement—the smallest twitch or peep emanating from a recruit. It seemed as though my DI had eyes on every side of his head. I couldn't help noticing how the cursing and threats were meshed together in unusual forms of foul language. It rolled off their tongues so fluently a person would think they had been preprogrammed for such expert profanity. At first, I could only catch a glimpse of my DI as he moved quickly up and down the line shouting orders. I could tell there wasn't a button, buckle, or insignia out of place. His shoes were shined like glass, and his uniform pressed to perfection. He was just as lean and mean as one would expect.

We were told to stand on painted yellow footsteps. Amazingly some recruits had difficulty accomplishing this simple task. Their inability to follow basic commands caused our DI to explode with anger. His face reddened and his neck muscles tightened as he explained in a textbook Marine Corps manner how undisciplined we were and how much we had to learn. As I stood stiff and attentive, I got the impression the apocalypse was imminent—at least on an individual scale.

The mosquito landing on my face had no regard for military etiquette. Having blood sucked out of my cheek was illustrative of the feeling I was getting from my DI as he immediately began to demolish the adolescent walls of safety I had constructed in my civilian life. His job was to tear us down and then build us back up in superlative Marine Corps fashion. He wasted no time in pursuit of that goal. The mosquito would not relent, so I smashed it on my cheek. The slap resonated and the apocalypse descended. Two DIs converged on my position and began shouting at the top of their lungs.

"What is your name, recruit!"

"Sir, recruit Dean, sir!"

"Recruit Dean, do you have any idea what you just did?"

"Sir, no sir!"

"You just killed your entire platoon! If you were in the jungle and did that, the Vietcong would know your position and kill you all!"

Our drill instructors had served two tours in Vietnam. They saw firsthand how a lack of discipline kills marines. In unison, their voices reverberated hitting the very core of our being as they ordered us to get on the ground and begin doing bends and thrusts. This is a wonderful Marine Corps exercise dreamed up to impact every single muscle, tendon, and fiber of the human body. From a standing position you quickly bend down on all fours and thrust your legs out and then in. We did this exercise over and over until our arms felt like rubber and our legs would barely thrust out. Once the DIs were satisfied we had no energy left in our bodies, we were told to stand at attention. I didn't know it at the time, but nearly half of all those standing wouldn't make it to graduation. I also didn't realize I would be the honor grad in our platoon.

Next they marched us into a one-stop, one-cut-fits-all barbershop. There were no hairstyle pictures and lists of prices on the walls. There were no old men sitting in chairs smoking cigars and chatting about the weather. The shop consisted of several chairs occupied by sad-looking recruits, multicolored mounds of hair on the floor, and barbers wielding clippers with the efficiency of Zorro. We all came out with our heads looking the same—bald.

After receiving a free marine recruit haircut, we were taken through a line and given our uniforms and seabag containing our equipment. Anyone who has ever been in the service doesn't forget the smell of piles of cotton uniforms, leather boots, and canvas bags intermingled with the clinical smell of waxed floors and cleaning solutions.

My experience in boot camp taught me many valuable lessons. Anyone who has been there will confirm there are two things those who earn the title of Marine never forget: 1) once a Marine—always a Marine, and 2) the name of their drill instructor. Both are engraved in my memory.

"Please fasten your seat belts."

I was awakened by an announcement from the flight attendant. Thankfully, I'd been able to get some sleep. As I adjusted my thoughts to my surroundings, I was also thankful I wasn't in Marine boot camp!

We were about to land in Milan.

2
CRIMES OF WAR

After retrieving my luggage I made my way to the rental car counter. The agent at the counter was doing his best in broken English to explain a rental agreement to, what appeared to be, an older tourist couple. The woman was neatly dressed and looking at a map. She jabbered to her husband about how to get to their first destination. The silver-haired man motioned to his wife to be still. After what seemed like twenty minutes, I had my keys and baggage in hand and was ready to get my car and get on the road. But the airport café was calling to me. I couldn't help thinking of a double shot of espresso. I would need an extra jolt to make the drive south to meet up with Pelley.

As I drove out into the countryside with an espresso in hand, I cracked the window and took a deep breath of fresh air. The cool air helped to further awaken my senses. I loved spring. Everything about it smelled fresh. Instead of the odor of a Sausage Finger's Polo cologne, I was now enjoying the aroma of blooming flowers and budding trees. The scenery was magnificent! I rolled by vineyards and Italian landscapes that would give any artist inspiration. On such a clear day I wanted to take it all in, absorbing every color and contour as I drove through places some only dream about seeing. After nearly two hours of driving, I made a right turn into a medieval looking town. The narrow streets were tricky to navigate. I had several near misses with scooters and pedestrians bravely weaving in and out between the cars.

As I maneuvered through the streets, I couldn't help looking up at the weathered stone faces peering down from within patches of paint on the buildings—faces reflecting hundreds of years of history. It seemed as though these faces came alive in the people as I heard folks talking and laughing, horns honking, and motorists yelling. Suddenly, the road spilled out into the piazza, which was now blocked by traffic. Even the pigeons scurrying on the ground, or the others circling in the air near a center fountain, seemed to play their part on cue to create a classic scene within the Italian piazza. Young children fed the pigeons as the other townspeople walked arm in arm enjoying the spring day.

I looked toward the hotel. Next to it was a small café, and there was Steve waving to me from one of the tables outside.

"Bonjour, Mike."

As usual, Steve sat with his back to the wall. This way he maintained a full view of all the activity in the square, as well as making sure no one was behind him.

"You need any help with your bags?" he asked.

"I've got 'em. I'm going to check in, and then I'll join you."

I was ready for another shot of espresso.

After checking in, and then making the trek to the third floor, I looked out the window of my room examining the piazza below. Next, I conducted a routine sweep of the room, checking every space and every exit. I quickly unpacked and got settled in, hanging my clothes in the closet. I didn't want to keep Steve waiting. It was only a few minutes until I was out the door, through the lobby, and out to the table where he was waiting.

"What's new, Steve?"

"All is well, but things are . . ."

There was an unusual expression on his face.

"What is it, Steve?"

He lit a cigarette and took a long drag. Raising his eyebrows, he glanced left and right. Then, leaning in closely, he said, "Things have started to heat up. I have some new information for you. But let's save it for later. I know you could use a nap. Can we meet at seven o'clock? I'll pick you up and we can drive out to a new restaurant I found. We'll have a glass of wine, and by then maybe you'll be ready for some good pasta."

As he left, I felt the flight, the drive, and the past twenty-four hours begin to crash in on me. Jet lag isn't just a catch phrase. I went back to the room to get some rest, although rest wouldn't come easy because now I had more questions than answers. My mind was spinning. I needed shut it down for a while. I looked up at the ceiling fan as I lay in bed. It wasn't long before its slow rotation made my eyelids feel like bricks. I drifted off into a deep sleep.

I awoke to the buzzing of my alarm clock. My three hour nap felt like thirty minutes. Steve would be in the piazza soon to pick me up. I turned on the water in the shower—not hot but warm—just enough to refresh me. After a shave I splashed on some cologne. My face burned a little as I walked to the closet and pulled out a clean, light blue polo shirt, less wrinkled than the others. The navy blue blazer with gold buttons I chose went well with my blue shirt, tan slacks, and loafers. After turning on the radio, and having one last look around the room, I headed for the elevator.

As the elevator doors opened into the lobby, I quickly scanned my surroundings but saw nothing unusual. Outside, the piazza was abuzz with activity. Children were chasing pigeons while parents pointed and laughed. Old men sat on the short wall around the fountain smoking and chatting. I looked at my watch. It was 6:59 PM. Sunset was still an hour away, and the sound of the noisy piazza echoed in my head.

"You ready, Mike?"

Steve was punctual.

"I'm ready to eat," I replied.

We didn't have to worry about beating the crowd to the local restaurant as most of the locals didn't eat until later in the evening. With both hands on the wheel, Steve maneuvered his way through town dodging both people and animals. I could tell something was bothering him. I could almost hear him thinking out loud. As we traveled through the village I found myself thinking of Sicily, where I had been stationed in the Navy many years ago. It was during those years my son was born in Naples. No wonder I felt a unique connection to my surroundings. My reminiscing was cut short as Steve simultaneously hit the brakes and horn, and then swerved to miss a mule cart along the road.

"Five minutes more," he said. "How ya feelin', buddy?"

I smiled. "I feel good, but I'm ready for that glass of wine and some Italian cuisine. How about you?"

"I'm ready for this rotation to end so I can get back to the States."

After climbing a winding hill we turned into the restaurant—a beautiful older building with a large patio overlooking a vineyard in the rolling hills below. The old stucco style blended perfectly with the droopy candles on the tables inside the restaurant and the dimly lit interior filled with Italian music. A red-checkered tablecloth brightened the room, giving it a warm and friendly feel. The ambience helped to ease my tension, and I began to relax.

"May we have that table in the corner by the window?" Steve pointed.

The waiter led us to the table we desired, poured water in our glasses, and then quickly brought us a basket of warm Italian bread. The candle flickered between us as Steve requested, "We'll have two glasses of your local red wine, and we'll need a few minutes before we order."

We waited for the waiter to return with the wine before we discussed business. I took a sip of wine and said, "Okay, Steve, what's heating up?"

The restaurant was empty, except for one couple on the other side of the room. We were safe. It was obvious the lovebirds across the room had eyes only for each other.

"I think we're getting close to the snatch, Mike."

The "snatch" Steve was referring to was the capture of a top war criminal. Our unit was working extremely hard in all facets of the operation. The unit's operations were always compartmentalized, and therefore we were only privy to information we needed to know from other sectors of the operation. Obviously Steve knew enough to know we were getting close.

Our job with the Unit was to make sure our unit had declonflicted airspace for classified special missions. Our job was very delicate considering we were not allowed to divulge the nature of our operation. Some may have assumed they knew what we were doing, but others were extremely curious and somewhat bothered by us being in the NATO operations room.

"It would be nice to wrap up the operation," I replied. "As much as I love Italy, I think I'm ready for South America. It's been awhile since I've seen those tango dancers."

The serious look returned to Steve's face as he continued.

"What I need to pass on is information concerning a NATO officer working in the Ops room who arrived last week," Steve explained. "You'll know him when you see him. He's the most arrogant looking person in the room. As far as I know, he's never done a rotation at this joint NATO Center. He's asking too many questions, Mike. I'm concerned. I've been told that he's asked others about air operations, and he wanted more specifics about why we needed airspace during military operations in this AO."

Steve stopped talking as the waiter made his way to our table. At that moment, however, my appetite was outweighing my curiosity. I ordered seafood pasta with mushrooms, lobster, and muscles—all caught fresh that day. Steve ordered pasta with Bolognese sauce.

"Steve, you'll never get away from meat sauce, will you?"

"It's what I like, Mike. You should know that by now."

Shortly after our dinner meeting, Steve was on his way home. His rotation had ended, and mine was just beginning. I was out of bed early the next morning. The sun rising over the landscape and shimmering off the fountain in the piazza was enough to make anyone appreciate life. I thought about the mission I was about to dive into as I opened my hotel window and took a deep breath of the cool morning air.

The Clinton administration and our European allies had adopted a new approach toward hunting war criminals. Their new plan included the Unit. Personnel involved in the NATO Ops Center were not aware of the secret activities of our unit. The Unit and its members were familiar only to others in the unit. Anytime we were involved in coordinated efforts with the interagency, coalition, SDF, or any other front line intelligence or counterterrorism organizations, we always worked concealed.

Prior to this coordinated effort, the allies had steered clear of attempting to arrest war criminals. The Joint NATO operation we were now engaged in was given the name Amber Star. Our overall mission was to snatch those accused of war crimes so that they could be brought before the International War Crimes Tribunal at The Hague. Radovan

Karadzic was at the top of our most wanted list. From 13 May, 1992, until he was driven from power in 1996, Karadzic had been the president of the Bosnian Serb administration in Pale, Bosnia Herzegovina. Under his command civilian gatherings were fired upon, killing thousands. He ordered civilians into detention facilities where their property was stolen, they were deprived of food and medical care, and detainees were subjected to torture including the rape of women and children. In all, many thousands of innocent people had been murdered.[7]

According to the Bosnian Book of the Dead—a casualty report published in 2007 by the Research and Documentation Center in Sarajevo—the Bosnian War claimed 350,000 recorded casualties including 97,207 deaths, 40 percent of whom were civilians. Of those killed the casualty report estimates that approximately 66 percent were Bosnian Muslims, 26 percent Serbs, and 8 percent Croats. In addition to those who lost their lives, countless more were traumatized in a program of torture, mass rape, forced labor, and confinement in concentration camps. The fate of Bosanski Samac—hometown of CJA client Kemal Mehinovic—captures the scale of devastation. Prior to the war, the town was home to 17,000 Bosnian Muslims and Croats. By May 1995, less than 300 of those residents remained. Such was the ruthless efficiency of the "ethnic cleansing."[8]

I was now working daily at the Operations Center which was not only highly secure, but lit up with multinational uniforms and crawling with high-ranking officials. I quietly went about my work of deconflicting Unit operations. Remembering Steve's concerns, I kept my eyes and ears tuned in to any extra efforts made by a certain NATO officer to extract information about our mission. Even though I had my own suspicions, I kept them to myself. As of yet, the line had not been crossed causing me to make a report. Our snatch efforts continued into the fall and through another rotation.

Mike Dean

Winston Churchill once said, "It's not what you make in a life, it's what you give in a life." For the soldier, the daily drudge of battle is only a means to an end—the end being victory bringing peace. A soldier, whether in uniform or civvies, is a patriot with a generous heart. On the east side of the magnificent shrine within the Indiana War Memorial it says, "The true patriot best supports his government by creating friendliness through kindness and generosity wherever fate may carry him." Wherever I went, I tried to portray these words to the best of my abilities.

As Christmas approached during my second rotation, I wanted to give something in return for the many blessings God had provided in my life. In most of the places I had traveled with the military, I always made an effort to find an orphanage or an organization through which I could somehow help others. With the possibility of this being one of my last missions with the Unit, I was determined it would be no exception when it came to giving to others.

"Count me in, Mike," an American serviceman responded to my suggestion.

I'd learned of an orphanage in the city not far from the NATO Operations Center that needed help providing Christmas presents for the children. I had no trouble recruiting volunteers and getting donations from personnel at the NATO Headquarters.

After collecting hundreds of dollars in donations, I had the fun of shopping for toys and many practical items the kids needed such as coats and gloves. This was a welcomed diversion from the high security and constant tension of our joint NATO operations. Over and over I found it to be true that it's always more blessed to give than to receive! I had discovered throughout my military career how the joy of giving also brings a sense of peace into a person's life. Bringing joy into someone else's life helps takes the focus off of one's own troubles. Since I couldn't be with my children at Christmas, it seemed fitting to bless other children who otherwise might not have many gifts.

After receiving a list from the orphanage, I went shopping at local stores and at a Base Exchange. Finding the gifts was easy enough. What would really make this effort a success would be having a Santa Claus to pass the gifts out to the children. I wanted this to be a memorable moment for the orphans.

"That's a lot of gifts. You must have a lot of kids," the cashier said with a big smile and broken English.

"These are for the children at the orphanage."

"That's so wonderful! Did you find everything you need?" she asked.

"Everything except a Santa to help me," I told her.

"Excuse me sir, did you say you need someone to play Santa?"

Our conversation had been overheard by an older gentleman standing nearby. As I looked at him, I realized I had found my Santa.

"Are you volunteering, sir?" I asked.

"I just happen to have a Santa suit. I would be glad to play Old Saint Nick for the orphans."

This particular gentleman was an American who had married an Italian woman and was living in Italy. He spoke the language fluently, which would make our visit even more memorable for the children as they sat on Santa's lap to receive their gifts. That Christmas helped us establish a good relationship with the orphanage, and we would make several more trips there during our operations in Italy. The military personnel involved grew quite fond of the kids, and I was always thankful for those moments of serenity in the sometimes unsettling world of special operations.

As the days went by in the NATO Operations Center I knew problems were developing. One revolved around the fact the former psychiatrist from Montenegro [Karadzic] had sought to resist responsibility for crimes carried out by his Bosnian Serb forces. As the world would find out after his capture, not only would he refuse to enter a plea concerning all the charges leveled against him (claiming the International Criminal Tribunal did not have the authority to prosecute him[9]), but he would also suggest that his arrest and trial were all part of a conspiracy against him.[10] Much of the current difficulty in tracking him down lay in the fact that after he was driven from power, the international authorities in Bosnia were supposed to avoid any contact with him. This made our groundwork extremely difficult.

Another thorn in our side was the French establishment and military bureaucracy being divided over what attitude to take in the Balkans. Questions had risen concerning the possibility of dubious ties by French officers with members of the Serbian Army. One example from a 1996 news report that aired on France 2's news program Envoye Special (Special Correspondent) alleged that the commander of UNPROFOR (United Nations Protection Force), General Bernard Janvier, took part in secret negotiations with General Mladic (Karadzic's right-hand man) and General Perisic, commander-in-chief of the Serbian Army. The French newscast reported how they negotiated to obtain the freedom of captured French UN troops in return for a promise not to order air strikes if Srebrenica were attacked.[11]

It wasn't long before an additional difficulty manifested, this one internal and more troublesome. We discovered that the security leak was known to have been close to Karadzic. This raised obvious concerns about possible leaks. Then, on top of apprehensions about the overall operation and the suspicion of leaks, we discovered that a bogus officer had been placed in support of Unit missions. Somehow he had won the confidence of the guards, after which he was able to find out what our team had discovered from weeks of monitoring communications—that Karadzic had vanished back across the border into Montenegro. Now we had more than a suspicion that our security leak had tipped him off.

The leak was reported to the secure elements in Washington D.C. Subsequently, both the American and British governments protested, but the outcry fell on deaf ears. However, one U.S. official was insistent when he said, "We know, definitely, that he passed information about NATO operations related to efforts to eventually get Karadzic."[12]

We knew we had to move away from working with those connected to the source of our leak. The Unit, along with Special Forces, began operations. We coordinated this new operation with our coalition partners. The intent, of course, was to keep the results from anyone connected to the source that had seemingly undermined our previous work. Day after day, the work of the Unit was tracking Karadzic while spooks gathered intelligence on the ground. With our American and British intelligence units teamed up, and while attempting to keep the undermining entity out of the loop, we were able to net a number of arrests of war criminals in British—and American-held sectors. During this same time, we also felt the need to track a female officer suspected of links to the Serbs. This officer's superiors continued to deny any wrongdoing, but when the Serbs were tipped off that their troops were about to be attacked from the air, the Unit knew who was to blame.

After much hard work, we were on the verge of snatching Karadzic who, coincidently, we believed was in a sector of Bosnia-Herzegovina friendly to the suspected source. This would be the culmination of our operations to this point. Unfortunately, this meant that those we suspected of leaking information could not be kept completely out of the loop. In order for our mission to be successful, we would need their support. This concerned us greatly given the problems we had had with the officers leaking information.

Once we had gathered the necessary intelligence and formulated the plan, we brought the suspected element in to help secure the location of the snatch. The plan called for sending in French Special Forces by helicopter to secure a villa where Karadzic was known to be, and disarm the police guards at the villa. Then U.S. SDF coalition force and our unit would move in to secure Karadzic. The men in French uniforms were now part of the team to carry out the plan.

I took a train to Venice for a much needed day off. After getting off the train I headed for the Piazza San Marco, better known to Anglophones as St. Mark's Square. What a magnificent site! It's bordered by historic buildings and represents the focal point of Venice's water transport system. Toss in some pigeons and outdoor cafés and you've got the scene Thomas Cortate described as "the fairest place of all cities." Cortate spoke his blessing in 1611, the year the King James Bible was first published. I found his words to be just as accurate near the end of the twentieth century.

I strolled down a side street just off the piazza. As I looked out at the canal, ornamented by an amorous couple boarding a gondola, I felt as though I was suddenly on a canvas being painted into the beautiful artwork of Venice. Continuing my stroll through the marvelous Venetian scenery, the aroma of Italian food in the air stirred up my appetite. I decided to stop at the next restaurant.

I hadn't walked more than a block when I found, what seemed to me, the perfect place. Their menu was listed on a board outside the entrance, and everything sounded wonderful. There were several outdoor tables with white tablecloths and fresh flowers. I would've preferred an outdoor setting, but all the tables were filled. The maître d' led me through the large entrance toward a second arched doorway into the back portion of the restaurant. From about the waist up on either side of the arched doorway, latticework extended to the ceiling and grapevines were woven throughout. The vines were sparse enough that I could see through portions of them to make out the faces on the other side. I requested a table in the rear of the restaurant, and sat with my back to the wall.

As I relaxed, the waiter brought water and bread. I took a casual look around. As I peered through the lattice, my eyes caught sight of an attractive female sitting alone. "Wait a minute," I said to myself. "It couldn't be . . ." She looked just like the woman who sat across the aisle from me on an earlier flight to Milan. What are the chances? Was it just a coincidence? I put my glasses on so I could get a better look at her face. As I peered through the latticework, I realized it wasn't a coincidence. I watched as a man walked up to her table. A twinge of adrenaline was accompanied by the ringing of the Pavlovian bell in my head. I couldn't believe my eyes! Sausage Fingers pulled back a chair and sat down across from the attractive blonde. I tried tuning in to their conversation, but from a distance it was barely audible. I could tell they were speaking French.

I remembered how on that particular flight, Sausage Fingers had conversed in German with the older gentleman sitting behind him. In the restaurant I watched as he put the same briefcase on the table. Once again I saw the "SLS" initials on the case. I had to know what was going on. When I saw them on the airplane they acted as though they didn't know each other; now they seemed very friendly. She scooted her chair back slightly as she crossed her long legs and took a cigarette out of her handbag. I could barely see the flame above Sausage Finger's hand as he reached over to light it. As the mysterious woman exhaled smoke, I leaned forward trying to catch any small piece of their conversation.

Some things in life are just too obvious to be considered coincidental. My curiosity wasn't a matter of transient paranoia. For me it was a matter of personal safety and the guarding of many months' worth of work that can be destroyed in a moment if a wrong step is taken. I moved slightly to my left behind a thicker portion of the grapevine as she looked through the lattice in my direction. I didn't want to be recognized. I was somewhat confident she hadn't noticed me or made the connection when I entered the restaurant.

I observed them as closely as I could until they left the restaurant. Many thoughts passed through my mind as I made a call to report the information. Even though I had not begun to tie all the threads together, I had to trust my gut instinct. I couldn't help but wonder if she was part of the connection through which we seemed to be experiencing information leaks. Sometimes it's like a puzzle, the pieces slowly being put together until the picture begins to take shape.

Everything in the Unit was compartmentalized. The information I was privy to was only what I needed to know. I knew I would never be supplied with any feedback concerning my suspicions of Sausage Fingers and the attractive blonde. Other factors, which I cannot disclose, led me to believe they had a direct connection to the security leaks. Hindsight has also given me a clearer picture. Publicly disclosed articles and reports revealed there were subversive attempts made by some to undermine our mission. Concerning the overall mission, and despite their attempts to subvert the capture of several war criminals, we still had many successes.

Radovan Karadzic was finally arrested in Belgrade on 21 July, 2008. He was extradited to the Netherlands and tried before the International Criminal Tribunal for the former Yugoslavia. Concerning the efforts of the Unit, General James L. Jones, Commander—US European Command, is quoted as saying: "The silent role in many of the snatch operations had been one of the greatest under-recognized success stories of our special missions in the Balkans."

3
SKYHAWK

My short break had ended after I returned from Italy. The afternoon sun garnishing the corn near the airfield made it look as though it had grown overnight. It was almost knee high. As I pulled into the airfield I noticed a car, and near it a small boy with his father. They were admiring a small Cessna 172 now on final approach.

As I glanced at the boy, I saw myself when I was his age. His eyes were wide open, and I knew he was dreaming of flying. I remembered how my father would take me to Greenwood Airport just outside of our small town. The fields around the airport looked the same. When I was that young I had no idea how aviation would one day play such an important role in my life—all the way from flight deck operations on the JFK to the position of Aviation Maintenance Officer in the 1st Calvary Division of the U.S. Army.

After parking in front of the airfield office next to the airport café, I sat for a moment remembering the day I soloed for the first time. I was only sixteen years old with eleven hours of flying time, and I had practiced several take-offs, landings, and emergency procedures when my instructor said (as we approached the FBO), "Let's make this a full stop and then let me out, Mike." He went on to say, "It's time to kick you out of the nest. Give me three full stop landings."

After taking off without my instructor in the plane, the butterflies in my sixteen-year-old stomach disappeared as I focused on flying. The first time you solo nearly everything you imagined could happen, or that you feared might happen, all goes right out the window. Your senses are tuned in as all your attention is on that first landing. I had altitude. I was downwind. My wings were level, and I made a quick scan for traffic and a quick scan of the gauges.

I radioed, "Greenwood traffic, Cessna 15 26 kilo, downwind for 18."

As I approached the midway point of the runway off to my left, I reduced power and flaps ten degrees. I turned left while watching my airspeed and instrument panel, and then scanned the horizon. Then, I made my next call.

"Greenwood traffic, Cessna 15 26 Kilo, turning base for 18."

Another ten degrees of flaps while checking airspeed and a quick scan and turn on final.

"Greenwood traffic, Cessna 15 26 kilo, turning final 18."

Ten more degrees of flaps while watching the airspeed. Over the runway, and then level off and slightly up on the yoke.

As I sat in the airfield parking lot reminiscing, I remembered the sense of joy and accomplishment when the tires of the plane touched the runway. The thoughts of my first solo flight disappeared as I saw my friend coming through the front door of the airport café to greet me.

"Mike . . . welcome back."

"Hello, Ed."

Ed Smiley was a retired Army lieutenant colonel who had been working for the special operations community for nearly half a decade before I met him, and was now a special operations program manager. He was the kind of man who everyone respected for his knowledge, his demeanor, and his service to the country. After graduating from Office Candidate School, he served with the Green Berets in Vietnam. Following Vietnam, he trained as a helicopter pilot, and then served in an Armored Division at Fort Hood, Texas. Later on, LTC Smiley also trained and was licensed to fly fixed wing aircraft in addition to helicopters.

Ed shared my love of flying. That's one reason our paths had crossed many times throughout the years. It's also why we chose to meet at the airfield café' for lunch, which was only known to a handful of local pilots and skydive junkies who frequented the airport on weekends. Our conversation quickly turned to business as we sat in a ragged booth overlooking the airfield. We discussed the best way to support operations in multiple locations worldwide, and how to improve upon a dynamic special operations support model—a model which exhibited the genius of Colonel Jerry King.

The use of special operations with integrated intelligence capabilities ramped up after the Desert One debacle. In April of 1980 an attempt was made by the U.S. Military to rescue fifty-three American hostages held in Tehran, Iran. The mission was codenamed Operation Eagle Claw, and sadly it resulted in the death of eight U.S. servicemen. Colonel Jerry King, a veteran of Army Special Forces, saw the reason for the catastrophe quite clearly. It stemmed from the military's inability to gather reliable intelligence quickly and effectively anywhere in the world. He was put in charge of a new top secret mission team, and was provided lots of manpower and new equipment to ensure that the next time they would have the right tools to do the job.

Oftentimes when clandestine military operations are discussed or written about, a lot of the attention is directed toward the personnel on the ground, units like the Navy Seals and other highly trained special operations units. Much of the reason for this lies in the fact that they are the front line units risking their lives at the direct point of contact with the enemy in the extremely hostile portion of the mission. At the same time, these front line special team members might also be the first to acknowledge how every compartment of a clandestine military operation is essential. Just as the highly trained sniper must continually be at the top of his game, so must the support personnel who are involved in garnering resources and gathering proper intelligence to ensure success of those on the ground.

In the early 1980's, the world was on the verge of the Internet age. Advancements in technology were increasing at a record pace. Concerning the development and use of technology, the military is usually eight to ten years ahead of the general public. Colonel King recognized the need for highly skilled intelligence and special operators throughout every sector of an operation. His visionary coalescence of old-fashioned and cutting-edge intelligence mechanisms paved the way for a multitude of successful clandestine operations.

In order to ensure the success of his new clandestine operation team, and in an effort to maintain total operations security, 200 million dollars was funneled out of official unclassified programs into top secret unofficial "black accounts" and used to procure the latest state-of-the-art communications and electronic warfare equipment for the Black Hawk long-range helicopters the mission planned to use.[13] This new unit's mission back into Tehran was called Operation Snow Bird. Subsequently, Colonel King became the founder of a new anonymous special operations organization known simply as the Unit.[14]

My job at the Unit required me to work with a variety of unique contractors to fulfill global unit support requirements. I loved my job and the chance to work with such high caliber people who were very mission focused. The fact is, a person was not able to work at this level unless they were in the top ten percent for the specific skill required.

Our Special Operations Teams were continually on the move. If they were not on a mission, they were engaged in training. The support we provided had to be timely and precise. If mistakes were made, people would die. At times the stress factor was high, but that's what we were trained for.

As Ed and I left the café, I received a call from my boss.

"Mike, we have a hot one. One of our assets at the south location is down and the mission is only forty-eight hours away. I need it fixed ASAP! Report back with your plan the minute you have it!"

"Got it boss—I'll get back to you within the hour."

Now I not only had a team in a hot spot, but the primary mission support asset was down. I called Tom, one of the enlisted special team members who had been with the unit for about eight years and told him to confirm we had the parts needed.

"This is too critical for an overnight shipment."

"How should we handle it, Mike?"

"Once you confirm we have the part, take it on the next commercial flight out," I told him. "Let me know when you're at the airport. I'll make sure the team knows your scheduled arrival."

I called the boss with the information, and then glanced at Ed who already knew what was happening—the process we discussed was working flawlessly.

"So much for an early night, Ed."

Ed smiled and said, "Gotta love it, Mike."

"You know I do, Ed! I wouldn't have it any other way!"

The next day started early with a meeting in D.C. It was almost 6 A.M. as I drove south on Interstate 95 from my home in Maryland. As I passed through Baltimore I looked over to my left at the gray Navy ship in port. My thoughts drifted from my meeting notes detailing our monthly aircraft status report, to the many years I served in the Navy and the moment I took my first step on the gangway of the JFK.

4

GANGWAY

Valor is needed in peace to sustain the unending war for truth and beauty which enrich life while they fortify against adversity.[15]

In February of 1980 I left Great Lakes Naval Training Center in North Chicago, Illinois, for Norfolk, Virginia. After transferring from the Marine Corps to the Navy, I was required to complete Navy boot camp. Thankfully, it was much easier than Marine Corps training. As I traveled to the East Coast, I thought about all the new experiences I would have serving aboard an aircraft carrier. I was ready for new challenges.

My new tour of duty would be aboard the *USS John F. Kennedy*, CV67. Prior to arriving in Norfolk, I had only seen pictures of aircraft carriers in magazines or on television. Until a person sees one up close, they cannot truly comprehend the sheer size of the ship. Commissioned in 1968, and christened by President Kennedy's daughter Caroline, it was America's largest fast attack carrier. She was an 83,000-ton ship, one fifth of a mile long, and her flight deck covered 4.5 acres with eighteen decks below. Measured from keel to mast top, it was as tall as a twenty-three story building and carried seventy-six aircraft. It was not only America's largest ship, but at the time it was the largest conventional (non-nuclear) ship in the world.

When you stand next to such an enormous vessel, you begin to understand why it's called a floating city. All together the JFK had approximately 5,000 personnel onboard. Over half were "ship's company"—crew members who remained onboard when the ship returned from deployment. The ship's crew didn't grow to 5,000 members until the carrier was being deployed and the squadrons of aircraft flew onboard.

As I approached the gangway the weight of my seabag made me wonder if I would make it to the top. The excitement of a new assignment and the thought that this would be my home for the next two years supplied the motivation as I walked up the gangway. When I reached the top I stopped, turned to the flag, saluted, and turned another 45 degrees to salute the Officer of the Deck.

"Sir, permission to come aboard."

Returning my salute, the officer replied, "Permission granted."

"Sir, Airman Dean reporting in."

"Welcome aboard, Airman." He signaled to the duty second class petty officer (equivalent to a sergeant in the Marine Corps). "Call an escort for the airman."

As the escort gave me a tour of the ship, many thoughts passed through my mind. I thought of the experiences that lay ahead, the amount of time I would be at sea, and the places I would visit that not so long ago I was only dreaming about. My tour of the ship came to an end as I was introduced to the officer in charge of flight deck operations.

"Airman, do you want to work in the hanger or on the flight deck?" asked the officer in charge.

"I'd like to work on the flight deck, sir."

Then he asked, "Do you like green water or blue water?"

Green water or blue water! What kind of question was that? His first question was easy, but I wasn't sure where he was heading with his second question. Later on I found out that "green water" is what you see when you're near a port, and "blue water" is the color of the ocean's deep waters. I suspected I was going to be harassed no matter how I replied. If I answered "green" he might say, "What'd ya mean? You don't want to go to sea?" I'd been in the military long enough to know that any answer I gave would probably be wrong. I took a chance.

"I like blue water, sir."

Sure enough, since my answer was blue water he replied, "What's the matter? You don't like coming into port?"

It didn't take long to learn that the classification of "airman" was broad and included a wide range of menial jobs. It certainly wasn't as detailed or specific, for example, as an aviation electrician (which I later became). My entry level status qualified me to handle a variety of jobs on or below the carrier's flight deck, and my request to work on top was granted.

Flight deck personnel received higher pay due to the hazardous surroundings. However, more pay wasn't my primary reason for wanting to work on the "roof" as they called it. I liked the idea of a fast-paced and more challenging environment. Every crew member's job on an aircraft carrier is essential—none lacked importance. At the same time, the flight deck was not only physically demanding, but most would've agreed it was more dangerous than other assignments. It was extremely noisy due to the combination of jet engines, loud speakers, and the constant flurry of activity when missions were in full swing. You had to keep your head "on a swivel" when working on the flight deck, otherwise you may not survive. The hazards also involved the rise and fall of the ship in high seas or a blast from a jet engine which would blow you off the ship as easily as flicking a fly off your arm.

For safety, organization, and communication purposes the various crews on the flight deck wore an assortment of brightly colored shirts to designate their area of operations. Because of noise and constant commotion, most of the communication was accomplished by hand signals and by recognizing the colors of the various departments. Yellow Shirts were the flight deck officers and plane directors; Blue Shirts were the flight deck crew; Green Shirts were in charge of catapult and arresting gear; Brown Shirts were squadron personnel, and in particular plane captains (no ship's company wore brown shirts); Red Shirts handled aviation ordinance; Purple Shirts were the aviation fuel crew (often referred to as "Grapes"); Checker Shirts were squadron maintenance and quality control; White Shirts were mail handlers; and White Shirts with a red cross were medical corpsman.

I was a Blue Shirt. We worked twelve hours on and then had twelve hours off. We pushed and pulled planes with "tugs" (small vehicles with a tow-bar), moving them back and forth from the flight deck to the hanger deck. We were also in charge of chocking plane wheels and then chaining them to the deck. We would also bring planes up on the elevators from below the flight deck. We even scrubbed the deck. Needless to say, we were the grunts.

During flight deck operations we frequently had several large chains hanging over our shoulders ready to move. After a plane would land, the Yellow Shirts (plane directors) would guide the pilot to a particular location on the deck. All of the flight deck crews were dependent upon each other. Even the pilots had to trust the Yellow Shirts' hand signals because all they could see from the cockpit was blue water. They trusted the Yellow Shirts not to guide them right off the edge of the ship. After the plane came to a complete stop, we launched into action, chocking the wheels and chaining the plane down.

Landing a plane on the deck of an aircraft carrier was not an easy task. The ship was gigantic to anyone standing up close or coming onboard. Yet, in comparison to the immensity of the ocean, and from an altitude of several thousand feet, it can appear as though you're trying to land a plane on a postage stamp. In addition to that dynamic, on a normal day at sea the ship would pitch up and down anywhere from ten to twenty feet. We had a great amount of respect for the pilots and their crews and the skill they displayed on a regular basis.

As I worked on the flight deck I observed how planes don't actually "land" on an aircraft carrier in the technical sense of the word. There wasn't a long runway for them to settle onto as one would witness in a normal aircraft landing during ground operations. During carrier operations, the aircraft is flown onto the deck; and in reality it's a high-speed arrival of tons of machinery while allowing for an immediate powered return to flight (called a "Bolter"). That's not to say they were reckless dives for the flight deck. Landings were an act of supreme piloting skill supported by a highly trained and professional group of people. A successful carrier landing was called a "trap" and was the ultimate test of nerve and flying skill for all the pilots.

Landing at night or in bad weather required even more skill. During "Blue Water Operations" (meaning far out at sea), if a pilot couldn't get aboard, his options were very limited and highly undesirable. Their pride and skill in bringing an aircraft onboard was continually on trial. Each trap was rated by a "Trap Rating System." Every trap was scored, and the target score was an "OK3" (3 indicating the third wire or arresting cable). Somehow this didn't seem fair to the pilot. I couldn't imagine after flying tons of aircraft at more than a hundred miles per hour onto a moving deck to simply be rated "OK." Still, I only towed them, chained them, and moved them up and down from the hangers to the flight deck.

My sleeping quarters were in the aft (rear) portion of the ship. Our racks (beds) were three high, each one smaller than a coffin. Mine was the middle rack, and underneath my mattress was a storage area. We were also directly beneath the flight deck and the retractable cables ("arresting gear"). When a plane landed, the pilot would lower a hook from the rear of the fuselage catching the arresting gear and "trapping" the plane. Once hooked, the cable would stretch to a certain point, and the tension would cause the plane to rapidly decelerate bringing it to a halt. After the aircraft was safely aboard, and after it raised its hook disengaging from the cable, the cable would retract sharply back to its original position and reset for the next landing.

The arresting cables operated on steam. If the flight deck was in full operation while you were trying to sleep, your lullaby was an orchestra of loud rhythmic clangs and bangs of metal-on-metal along with the release of steam and the roar of jet engines in the background.

Eventually your body becomes conditioned to sleep through the noise. At that point you're somewhat convinced you can sleep anywhere!

After leaving Norfolk we sailed near the Caribbean for our "pre-deployment ops." These were "work-ups," or exercises to test and certify our overall skills and readiness. I was not only new to Navy deployment operations, but to the sea itself. These are very memorable moments in anyone's military career. I was beginning a new chapter in my life—learning new skills, building camaraderie with new people, and seeing places I had only dreamed about.

As we began our work-ups, I focused on learning as much as I could, as fast as I could. Military ops are demanding, and you're allowed very few mistakes. Oftentimes when I would take a break from working on top, I would go down the ladder to a catwalk a half deck below and look out over the ocean, finding it to be a great stress reliever. Sometimes I would even go there on my day off. It was breathtaking to look out at the enormity of the ocean. My mind would try to comprehend what my eyes were taking in, but it was impossible to fathom the amount of space consumed by the water. When I gazed at the ocean I was not only overwhelmed with feelings of awe, but I was almost hypnotized by the shimmer extending to the horizon. As the stress of the day subsided, I began to sense a strange type of loneliness in the realization that I was just a tiny speck on a giant globe.

"Hey, Dean," another airman said one day as he broke into my relaxed state of mind.

"What do you need?"

"I'm looking for someone to trade shifts with me."

"I'll think about it."

I was hesitant to agree to trade shifts during work-ups as I needed to remain in a steady routine and become proficient at my job. I thought about it for a few days, and finally agreed to trade places with my fellow Blue Shirt. When our day to trade shifts arrived, I stood on the catwalk enjoying a little solitude compliments of my fellow airman. Solitude, that is, relative to being on a ship with 5,000 others. In the background I could hear the roar of jet engines as another flight operation got underway; catapults were sending F-14s into flight.

Launch and Recovery Operations on an aircraft carrier must be the world's most unique aviation setting. During my initiation to the flight deck (which included hazing) I was continually amazed at what took place. The operations unfolded with beautiful precision. Some have even referred to it as a ballet of sorts; an intricate dance of moving machines and people. A less-than-perfect performance in a civilian ballet will result only in poor ticket sales and bad reviews. But, a poor performance in the "ballet" of Flight Deck Operations would likely result in an accident with injuries, or even death. I was reminded over and over how the flight deck is one of the world's most dangerous places to work. It's unforgiving; the pace is demanding; and injury or death is always lurking. Our Flight Operations Cycle required fourteen, sixteen, and sometimes eighteen hours or more of intense focus interrupted only by hectic minutes of maintenance and repair between launch and recovery. All of our efforts were geared toward one goal—getting the Navy's big guns in the air.

After several landings, the soothing effect of the ocean and the wake of the ship were suddenly interrupted by a loud commotion on the flight deck. I ran across the catwalk and quickly climbed the ladder to see what had happened. During its landing, an A-7E Corsair broke through an arresting cable. The three-inch steel cable snapped, slinging it violently in two directions. The odds of this occurring were remarkably minimal, but if it ever did it was one of the most treacherous scenarios on the flight deck. The uncontrolled whip of the cable smashed through the tails of three SH3 helicopters, and severed both legs of a Green Shirt working nearby.

As medics hustled onto the flight deck, my eyes began to focus painting a clearer picture of the horrible scene. It was then that I saw something I wish I could erase from my memory. I saw the head of the airman I had traded shifts with rolling on the deck. He had been sitting on a tug when the cable broke. Within seconds the thick wire severed his head and his body slumped over the tug bleeding profusely. In all, there were two casualties and three injured that day.

The planes still in the air were kept in a holding pattern while flight deck crews moved quickly to clean up the mess. The deck of the John F. Kennedy had four arresting cables—planes would continue to land once the deck was cleared of debris. It was during times like this I learned how we had to put our personal feelings aside and concentrate on all that needed to be done. I had to ignore the massive amount of blood, and the nightmarish scene of a headless body and a man missing both legs, in order to clean up the scene and continue on with the mission at hand. As heartless as it sounds, that's the reality of military preparedness and operations. This was as real as it gets! The medics evacuated the injured personnel while we cleared the deck.

Sometimes the impact of a horrible event doesn't sink in until days afterward. I couldn't help thinking how I might have been dead if I had been working that shift. Then, I would feel guilty for thinking such thoughts. It's a vicious cycle. At some point I had to just let it go. What many servicemen and women will take away from these moments is a greater understanding of what it means to be on the front lines of military service. To one degree or another, all who serve in the armed forces have to come to grips with the hard truth that their existence on this earth might be brief. It could end in a moment of time and they may never see death coming their way.

After pre-deployments ops, we began our tour of the Med and IO. Though the pattern of life on an aircraft carrier takes a little time for a newcomer to adjust to, eventually you succumb to it. Psychologically, it takes some time to settle in to the idea of being in the middle of an ocean and thousands of miles away from land. All you see for weeks on end is water, birds, and fish. On one deployment we were at sea fifty-three days before having a port call.

When we weren't on duty we could take advantage of the ship's workout facilities, library, or I could just relax in the rack. The JFK, though nothing like a cruise ship, had something happening every hour of the day. Even the chow hall was open twenty-four hours. They served three regular meals, but if we were hungry at other times the mess hall had a "quick line" where crew members could get pizza, hamburgers, and other fast food. We even had our own television and radio station onboard—WJFK. The ship's TV had shows and movies, and it kept us updated about the next port call. Some weren't able to leave the ship, either because they were on duty or possibly because they were in some sort of trouble.

The POD (plan of the day) would tell us what was going on within the ship on any given day. It would list the uniform of the day, various shift activities taking place, what personnel needed to report to the various compartments, whether there was a command ceremony planned, and even the next port call. When the ship entered a port of call, the MWR (moral welfare and recreation) would sponsor tours for a minimal cost to Navy personnel. This was my opportunity to see foreign places. I took advantage of as many as I could.

During our deployment in the Med we had what was called a Tiger Cruise. During this cruise, the crew was allowed to invite their fathers or sons aboard to spend some time at sea observing the ship's operations. Our family members found out how everyone aboard ship must participate in certain types of readiness training. For instance, all the crew must be trained in—and participate in—fighting fires. In the middle of the ocean, everyone is part of the fire crew, and everyone had to be trained for an attack. And we all had to be trained for a fast accounting of the crew in the event of a man overboard. If a man did go overboard, a siren would sound requiring a speedy muster (a gathering into formations) to find out who was missing.

During the Tiger Cruise we showed off our skill with a muster of the entire crew in only minutes. We were accustomed to these types of drills. Men moved fluently from every compartment of the ship to their assigned locations. My father (who came with me on a cruise) was astounded that 5,000 men could be assembled and accounted for in such a short amount of time. Unfortunately, however, the drill my father witnessed wasn't just a drill. Two men were missing! Typically if a man went overboard, and if he survived the eighty-foot drop to water, he would inflate his survival vest. This vest included a flashing light as well as a dye that went into the water to aid the rescuer in locating the individual. Sadly, during this drill there were no flashing lights and no visible signs of men in the water. The two men were never found.

After the muster was over, we were told a few details of what happened. Two crew members were bringing a plane up on an elevator during rough seas. An enormous wave came over the elevator deck and slapped the two crew members off the elevator and into the ocean as if they were specks of dust. The men were listed as "Missing at Sea." I felt sorry for their families. It must be extremely difficult for the loved ones of those missing at sea not to have the closure of a body being returned to the States, or a graveside service where they can actually bury the body of their family member. It's bad enough when a soldier is missing in action during wartime. But this was peacetime. I took solace in the truth that God knows all those who have perished from this earth. If one sparrow cannot fall without the Lord knowing, then it was reassuring to know He could reach down into the lives of those experiencing such a loss and provide comfort. That horrible incident served to drive home the fact that on a Navy vessel there is ever-present danger. We had to stay alert.

All in all, life on the JFK was as exciting as one would imagine. The friendship of fellow sailors, the long hours of work, the opportunities to study and learn new things, all of this helped the days and weeks pass by more quickly. Most importantly our sense of duty kept us in tune with the task at hand. As for me, the port calls of the Mediterranean and Indian Ocean helped fulfill a portion of my life's ambitions.

5
PORT CALLS

One of the main reasons I transferred to the Navy had to do with my desire to see the world. I was fascinated by foreign lands—including the people and the history. Sometimes I felt a little out of sync with many of the sailors my age. Much of their interest in foreign lands seemed to be centered upon locating those of the opposite sex as well as the local pubs. Being a young sailor, I wasn't opposed to indulging in an adult beverage once in a while. But, I didn't want to look back with regret not having taken advantage of the opportunities I had to see many of the places I had previously only daydreamed about.

Our first port call in the Mediterranean was Malaga, Spain, a town located along the Costa del Sol ("coast of sunshine"). As we sat in the harbor waiting for the liberty boats to take us ashore, I thought of how many sailors before me had visited these faraway places. I talked with other crew members about what there was to do on shore.

"Mike, there are two things to make sure you do while you're here," one of my fellow sailors advised. "The first thing you have to do is see a flamenco show, and the second is to have some paella."

My shipmate had been to Malaga many times, and I trusted his advice.

"I'll do that," I replied.

Paella was originally a Spanish laborer's meal that was cooked over an open fire in the fields. I was nearly salivating as my friend described the uniquely Spanish dish.

"Mike, paella is amazing! It's made with fresh vegetables, rice, seafood, and incredible spices."

"Stop! That sounds so good! I'm gonna swim to shore if you don't quit!"

Flamenco shows would also be a new experience for me. I remembered seeing one on TV when I was a kid. I could picture the intense guitar strumming and gypsies dancing. The music seemed to erupt from within their souls. I remembered watching as their boots pounded the floor and they clapped their hands while staring deep into each other's eyes. I couldn't wait to see a show performed by some of the best dancers in the country. Considering the way I had always loved to wander, along with my present desire to see the world, I often felt like I had some gypsy in my blood.

The significance of Malaga, Spain, in my life was that it represented the first country I'd visited other than Canada. I had gone from being a teenager staring out the window of a classroom in high school, while daydreaming about faraway places and experiencing life in other cultures, to being on the brink of visiting as many places outside the U.S. as would be possible during our Med/IO tour.

As much as I enjoyed the friendship of my shipmates, I quickly left their company to find a bus or a train, or any other type of transportation into the Spanish countryside. As I suspected, many of my shipmates headed for the first bar they could find. The last thing I wanted to do was spend my time in a foreign country going from one local bar to another. I was going to do my best to see the real country—not the tourist traps. I wanted to meet real people, not just the ones who wanted to separate sailors from their American dollars. I wanted to learn something about the country's history. Getting off the beaten path, and seeing the country on my own, also meant I had to find someone who spoke some English.

I found help with directions to one of the most memorable moments of the port call in Spain, traveling to Granada to see the Alhambra Palace. What an amazing sight! It sits on a hill overlooking the city. Some poets have described it as "a pearl set in emeralds," in allusion to the color of its buildings and the woods around them. Alhambra was exactly the type of sight I desired to see. I was in awe of the architecture of this 1100-year-old structure. As one writer put it: "The romantic imagination of centuries of visitors has been captivated by the special combination of the slender columnar arcades, fountains, and light-reflecting water basins found in those courtyards—the Lion Court in particular; this combination is understood from inscriptions to be a physical realization of descriptions of Paradise in religious poetry."[16]

I also spent some time in museums, local restaurants, and small villages. Before leaving Spain, I did eat paella and see flamenco dancers. It was all just as wonderful as I imagined!

Our next port call was in Toulon, France. Located in the west of the French Riviera, and unlike most of the towns in France, Toulon is not crossed by any big river. The economy relies upon the presence of the French naval base that creates thousands of direct and indirect jobs. Like so much of France, the history and ancient architecture were stunning! When you first arrive you see the port and its promenade. There are usually souvenir shops, coffee shops, and restaurants. On the port square I stared up at the well-known statue of the Spirit of Navigation pointing to the sea.

Place Puget, in the historical center, is the ancient center of the town. In the center of Place Puget is a fountain built in 1780 with a sculpture of three dolphins, now completely covered in ivy. Near Place Puget is Saint Marie de la Seds Cathedral, began in the eleventh century but never finished. I felt an odd sensation standing in places where civilizations and ancient governments and militaries fought over land, and where sailors looked out at the sea surmising that the world was flat.

Toulon met all of my high expectations. Memories of these cities and their architecture are etched in my mind. I knew they would be. The world is a fascinating place. I believe everyone needs to see these places or experience them somehow—even if only on documentary films or encyclopedic entries. To plant my feet in places that are thousands of years old, and where such a great amount of world history has taken place, was more than my mind could comprehend. I simply did the best I could to soak it all in.

After leaving the Mediterranean, we headed for the Suez Canal. What a drastic difference in culture from that of Spain and France! Of course this canal is one of the most important waterways in the world because it allows ships to pass from the Mediterranean to the Persian Gulf and into the Indian Ocean without going south around the tip of Africa. The number of trade ships passing through is staggering.

I also found its history to be interesting. In the late 1700s Napoleon believed if he could build the canal, the French could control trade so that the British would have to pay them dues to transport goods from India and the Far East. Studies for Napoleon's canal plan commenced in 1799. However, a miscalculation in measurements purported the sea levels between the Mediterranean and the Red Sea would make it unachievable and canal construction stopped. Officially completed in 1869, the canal is 101 miles long and cost $100 million to build. In

1875, debt forced Egypt to sell its shares in ownership of the Suez to the United Kingdom. Later, an international convention in 1888 made the canal available for all ships from any nation to use.

Unlike most canals, the Suez has no locks because the Mediterranean Sea and the Red Sea's Gulf of Suez have approximately the same water level. For us, it took around eleven to sixteen hours to pass through the canal. We were required to travel at a low speed to keep the ship's wake from eroding the canal.

As we slowly made our way through, I couldn't get over how small the waterway was in respect to the size of the JFK. Compared to the ship, it almost seemed as if we were on a small river or creek. When I looked off the top of the carrier, all I could see was land. There were moments when my eyes were playing tricks on me making it seem as though we were sailing across dry land. A lot of people on camels were watching the gigantic ship travel through the canal, putting the crew on high alert. In a confined area at such a low speed, we were an extremely large target for an attack.

After sailing out of the canal into the Indian Ocean, we remained at sea for over fifty days before arriving at another port. The Indian Ocean was an unbelievable expanse of water. Once again I was reminded of how small we are on the earth in comparison to the vastness of the oceans.

(What I'm going to describe next has nothing to do with port calls. It actually occurred while at sea. However, it is an event that multitudes of sailors have experienced, and those who have will never forget.)

In the U.S. Navy, a time-honored ceremony takes place when a ship crosses the equator. With few exceptions, those who have been inducted into the "mysteries of the deep" by Neptunus Rex and his royal court count the experience as a highlight of their naval career. Members of the Neptunus Rex's party usually include Davy Jones, Neptune's first assistant, Her Highness Amphitrite, the Royal Scribe, the Royal Doctor, the Royal Dentist, the Royal Baby, the Royal Navigator, the Royal Chaplain, the Royal Judge, Attorneys, Barbers, and other names that suit the party. All of those involved are dressed for the part. It has the appearance of a cartoonish looking adult costume party with homemade costumes including paper crowns, mop heads for wigs, and scepters wrapped in aluminum foil. It's somewhat reminiscent of a college toga party and hazing. Many of the initiates are dressed in white t-shirts and pants and wearing their skivvies over their pants.

Officially recognized by service record entries (indicating date, time, latitude and longitude), the crossing of the equator involves elaborate preparation by the "shellbacks" (those who have crossed the equator before) to ensure the "pollywogs" (those who are about to cross the equator for the first time) are properly indoctrinated. All pollywogs, even the commanding officer if he has not crossed before, must participate.

After "crossing the line," pollywogs receive subpoenas to appear before King Neptune and his court. Some wogs may be interrogated by King Neptune and his entourage. This may involve the use of "truth serum" (a mixture of hot sauce and aftershave) as well as whole uncooked eggs being put in the wogs' mouth. During the ceremony, the pollywogs undergo a number of increasingly embarrassing ordeals. Some of these ordeals include wearing clothing inside out and backwards, crawling on hands and knees on nonskid-coated decks, swatted with short lengths of fire hose, locked in stocks and pillories and pelted with mushy fruit, locked in a water coffin of salt water and bright green sea dye (fluorescent sodium salt), crawling through chutes or large tubs of rotting garbage, and kissing the Royal Baby's belly coated with axle grease and hair chopping. All of this hazing is done largely for the entertainment of the shellbacks.

Once the ceremony is complete, a pollywog receives a certificate declaring his new status. Another rare status is the golden shellback, a person who has crossed the equator at the 180th meridian (the International Dateline). The rarest shellback status is that of the emerald shellback, which is received after crossing the equator at the prime meridian. When a ship must cross the equator reasonably close to one of these meridians, the ship's captain will typically plot a course across the Golden X so that the ship's crew can be initiated as golden or emerald shellbacks.

After becoming a shellback, and while in a port of call during our deployment in the IO, I went on a safari in Mombasa, Kenya, and took a hot air balloon ride near the base of Mount Kilimanjaro and out over Tsavo National Game Park. My eyes were wide open as I looked in amazement at things I had only read about in *National Geographic*. Tsavo East National Park is Kenya's largest national park covering an area of 11,700 square kilometers. You see everything from great herds of elephants, antelope, hippos, black rhinos, lions, and giraffes to buffalo and a host of birdlife. The major attractions in the park are the Yatta plateau, Lugard Falls, Aruba Dam, Mudanda Rock, and many rock and cave paintings.

Mombasa is steeped in history, and yet it's also a cosmopolitan port town. I found the true heart of Mombasa in the exotic old town, among the narrow winding streets and Arab architecture. The air is heavy with the scent of spices. Women were wearing the traditional buibui as they filled the narrow streets and busy marketplace. The streets were alive with the bright colors of the traditional coastal khanga and kikoy, the all-purpose wraparound cloth worn by both men and women. At the water's edge is Fort Jesus, an imposing fort standing watch over the harbor. The high gun turrets, battlements, and underground passages of the sixteenth-century fort were the center of a historic struggle for control of the Kenyan coast between the Portuguese army and the Shirazi Arabs.

After Kenya we sailed west. Our next port call was Perth, the capital of Western Australia. It is the most isolated capital city of over one million people in the world, closer to Jakarta and Singapore than Adelaide, the nearest other Australian city.

Of course I found the history of Perth very interesting. It revolves around British settlers establishing a free settler colony in 1829 as part of the Swan River Colony. From 1850, an influx of convicts boosted the size of the colony and their labor helped shape the early architecture of the city. Then, in the 1890s, the discovery of gold triggered a boom which, along with subsequent mineral discoveries, was a key to the city's economical growth.

Perth had all the classic Australian sights. It had semi-wild kangaroos in the Pinnaroo Valley Memorial Park, along with Australian Rules Football every weekend between March and August. Perth boasted of having some of the country's best beaches, and of course there were the local pubs, restaurants, and shops.

As I stepped down the ship's gangway at Perth, I didn't realize I was about to encounter something I had not experienced in any other port. This port call would be one of the most memorable.

"Hello, young man," an elderly couple greeted me.

"Hello," I answered (not thinking much of it at the moment). The crowd was large, and I assumed the couple was looking for friends or family members.

"Have you been at sea very long?"

They seemed very nice. I still couldn't determine whether they were just making small talk, or whether they were really interested in my time at sea.

"We've been in the Indian Ocean a little over fifty days," I answered.

"Have you been to Australia before?" they asked.

"No, I haven't."

"It's a wonderful place to visit. Do you have an idea what you're going to do in Perth?"

"Well, I want to see as much of the people and sights as I can." The conversation was pleasant, but I still couldn't understand why they were so interested in me.

"Young man, I'm a veteran of World War II," the man began to explain, "and my wife and I like to show our appreciation for the U.S. military in any way possible. Would you allow us to show you some of the sights?"

I was surprised by such an offer! "Sure, that would be great," I replied.

"We'd also like to invite you to stay with us for a few days, and we can be your personal tour guides. How's that sound?"

I had never encountered this type of hospitality. Out of all the people on the dock, which mostly consisted of women desiring to meet an American sailor, I happened to be the one this older Australian couple struck up a conversation with.

My hosts took me to several museums and local shops; they told me many details and stories about Australia; and they introduced me to the famed vegemite sandwich. They loved horseback riding, and had horses in a stable near their house. One of my fondest memories of Perth is when they took me horseback riding along the beach.

After leaving Australia, we sailed northeast toward Oman. We were off the coast just before Easter Sunday. When Sunday arrived I went up to the flight deck at sunrise. As I looked out at the sea I saw a whale, the first time I had witnessed such a sight. An odd feeling of loneliness came over me (probably due to the calm seas) while at the same time a feeling of awe at the dramatic sight of a whale swimming within view. There were no flight deck operations underway that would have scared off this type of marine life. I turned around to get the attention of anyone who might be nearby, but I saw no one else on the deck. For me, it was a memorable Easter sunrise. I stood there watching a whale enjoying the open sea with the coastline of Oman in the background. It reminded me of the magnificence of God, and how His creation continues to reveal His majesty and power.

Serving aboard the JFK provided some of the most memorable moments of my military career. The ocean, the ports of call, and the experiences aboard ship are all indelibly etched in my memory. Yet, it was during that time that I sensed my life heading in a different direction. I desired to be upwardly mobile, but not simply for the sake of upward mobility. Continually chasing higher rank and privilege was not at the core of my decision making or the yearning I had for change. I wanted to learn more. I wanted to find that place where all of my skills would continue to be developed and in full use. I wanted to become the person God had created me to be.

I was confident that I needed to continue on in my military service. On 29 March, 1983, I raised my hand in front of the Secretary of the Navy, John F. Lehman Jr., aboard the JFK and swore to uphold and defend the Constitution of the United States as I reenlisted. I didn't realize at the time how the Navy would not be where I would find long-term fulfillment in my military service.

6

A TIME OF TRANSITION

"Let's hear it for a legend; a man who has been giving his time for forty years to entertain U.S. troops all over the world . . . Mr. Bob Hope!"

Thunderous applause rose from the crowd as the noted comedian took the stage.

"The last time I played golf with President Ford he hit a birdie—and an eagle, a moose, an elk, an aardvark," Hope said in his iconic style. "But, Ronald Reagan . . . now he's not a typical politician. He doesn't know how to lie, cheat, and steal. He's always had an agent to do that."[17]

Along with Bob Hope, we were entertained by Sammy Davis Jr., Jonathan Winters, Brooke Shields, and Bobby Goldsboro, who had come to Pensacola Naval Air Station to do a USO show. I was fortunate enough to be sitting in the front row and afterward to be able to meet Bob Hope.

When I reenlisted, I was given a choice of my next duty station. In May of 1983 I chose an assignment at the Naval Air Station at Pensacola, Florida—the cradle of Navy aviation. It's where Navy pilots and aircrew receive their training, and the home of the famous Blue

Angels. I was assigned to the HC16 helicopter unit. These were UH1N Helicopters whose primary mission was search and rescue.

Up to this point, I was self-taught concerning most aspects of aircraft mechanics. While on the JFK I had some on-the-job training in aviation electronics while at the same time I was taking courses on aviation airframe and power plant maintenance. After being reassigned to Pensacola Naval Airbase, I continued to work on helicopters as an aviation electrician. I also continued taking courses in order to obtain my FAA airframe and power plant license.

Pensacola Naval Airbase provided many learning opportunities. Like all of my other military experiences, I didn't realize as they were unfolding how each played a role in preparation for future positions. Part of the excitement I found was in accompanying helicopter crews on search and rescue training flights. Even though I wasn't a certified rescue diver, the crew allowed maintenance personnel to fly with them. What a great feeling flying in a UH1N rescue helicopter with the side door open and my feet hanging out as I watched the scenery go by along the coast of Florida!

When I wasn't on duty I worked at the Navy Flying Club. This helped me in my pursuit of an FAA license and allowed me to complete the flight time I needed for my pilot's license. I also joined the yacht club (though I didn't even own a rowboat). I volunteered to help with anything they needed just so I could learn how to sail. I loved sailing and had always been fascinated by the ocean. Sailing on the JFK as part of a 5,000-member crew was exciting, but I also desired to sail on small boats as part of a small crew. The average sailboat was between 24 to 50 feet. While helping out, I was able to become a pretty good sailor. The Yacht Club also had a lot of yacht races, and after getting to know the members I was asked to be a deckhand to assist with the races.

"Mike, what are your goals? What's the future hold for you?" Chuck asked me one day.

Chuck was a former F-14 fighter pilot who had made quite a bit of money in the stock market. He thought about making a career of military service, but then decided to pursue another dream. While unmarried, Chuck was going to spend the next two years of his life sailing around the world.

"I have a lot of dreams and goals, Chuck. Some of them I've already accomplished," I answered. "But, there's a lot more I plan on doing."

I had met Chuck at the Yacht Club, and volunteered to help him prepare his 48-foot boat for his global sailing adventure. It took us three months to get it ready.

"Don't ever forget, Mike, you can accomplish anything you desire if you keep pursuing your goals."

Chuck was one of those rare people we meet who inspire us with their words, and with their very lives. A person who actually means what he says, who passionately pursues his dreams, and who is unselfish enough to take the time to inspire others along the way. People like Chuck are not jealous of others accomplishing their dreams because their desire is for everyone to succeed.

I had the privilege of helping him as he launched out to realize his dream of sailing around the world. He sent me postcards from many of the stops he made to resupply his boat. Unfortunately, he ran aground in the south Pacific after setting his boat on autopilot. When the boat started taking on water, he floated for a day, and then thankfully he was rescued by a freighter. Still, Chuck's words and efforts were an inspiration in my life. He inspired me to dream big and never give up.

Handwritten postcard from Tahiti:

> Pos = Poste Restante
> Papeete Tahiti,
> French Polynesia
>
> Hi Mike,
> Hope everything going well for you. The boat & I are holding up very well. My liver is getting quite a workout! The sailing has been mostly fairly good, some light (no) air & headwind Panama → Galapagos but had a great 21 day passage to the Marquesas. My Seattle friend will meet me here in a few weeks & will sail to Tahiti. We should be there early in Dec. Take care
> Chuck L—
>
> Mike Dean
> HC 16 Avionics
> NAS Pensacola FL
> 32508
> USA

Even though I had a passion for aircraft mechanics and flying, I also desired to move into the officer ranks. I took any opportunities I had to continue my education and achieve certifications. My time at Pensacola was not only a great environment to live and serve in, but most of what I learned there would play a key role in the events which would occur later when I was selected for the Unit.

After three years at Pensacola I was reassigned to the HC4 (Helicopter Combat Support Squadron 4) at the Naval Air Station in Sigonella, Sicily. HC4 was the home of the Navy's Sikorsky CH-53E Super Stallion helicopters. The CH-53E Super Stallion was designed to change the face of helicopter logistics support forever. With twice the lifting capacity and a far greater range than any of its predecessors, the CH-53E was the most capable heavy-lift helicopter in the NATO inventory. Recognizing its potential for fleet support, the U.S. Navy commissioned its first—and only—dedicated CH-53E squadron on 6 May, 1983.

After arriving in Sigonella, I discovered there was no housing on base so I rented a house about thirty miles off base for my family, which now consisted of my wife, two kids, and another child on the way. We settled down in the city of Motta Sant'Anastasia. Motta was located at the foot of Mount Etna, the highest active volcano in Europe. While speaking to the landlord, I learned that the Mafia was alive and well in Sicily.

"Mr. Dean, you must pay the extra each month," the landlord informed me.

"Why?" I asked. After all, I was U.S. military personnel. How was the Mafia going to extort money out of me?

"Mr. Dean, please. Unless you want your house broken into, you must pay the extra each month. It is true for everyone who rents here."

I had moved onto an island in the Mediterranean that had recently experienced what was referred to as the Second Mafia War, a conflict within the Sicilian Mafia which had mostly taken place in the early 1980s. The history of the Sicilian Mafia was replete with conflicts and power struggles, but the violence was typically localized and short term. However, the Second Mafia War—which some even called The Great Mafia War, or the Mattanza (Italian for The Killing)—involved the entire Mafia and radically altered the power balance within the organization.[18]

Sicily was a hotbed of Mafia extortion and killings. The Second Mafia War involved a staggering amount of violence, with upwards of a thousand homicides. The dates of the war are sometimes given as 1981 to 1983, but while the majority of the violence did occur during these years, the first shots had been fired in 1978, and the instigators and eventual victors had been preparing their strategy some years before. Similarly, the victors dragged the killing out until the end of the 1980s as they disposed of their allies.[19]

Not long before I arrived in Siganella, a man named Pippo Fava was killed while waiting to pick up his granddaughter who was rehearsing a part in a theatre comedy. Fava was the editor of the newspaper in Catania, and an outspoken anti-Mafia activist. The week before he was killed he had been a guest on Enzo Biagi's national TV show where he denounced the sway the Mafia held in parliament. Also, while I lived there a judge in Palermo was killed, his body mutilated, and his two grandkids shot in the backseat of his car for sentencing a Mafia family member to prison. Thankfully, we never witnessed any of these situations firsthand.

On the positive side, Sicily had incredible scenery and scores of historical sites, including ancient Greek ruins. While stationed in Sicily I was also able to embark on many other port calls via the CH-53E Super

Stallion helicopters. The squadron I was attached to was called upon to fly mail and supplies to the aircraft carriers and other ships within the region. I flew with the crews to Izmir, Turkey, as well as Malaga, Marbella, and Palma de Mallorca, Spain. But out of all the great experiences I had in Sicily, the most important was the birth of my son.

I spent several years as a helicopter mechanic in Pensacola, Florida, before being assigned to HC4 in Sigonella. The Navy had provided a solid foundation in my military career—aviation mechanics in particular. I was approaching my eighth year in the Navy while at HC4, and had risen to the rank of Petty Officer Second Class. Though I was on the list for promotion to Petty Officer First Class, I began to realize I would not go much further in my current job position. I wasn't qualified to become a Naval Flight Officer (due to my eyes), and I knew I had reached a point of acceptance or transition. Not being the type of individual who accepts immobility in an amiable fashion, I needed a new road to travel. I still had a desire to move into the officer ranks. The question was, should I stay in the Navy while pursuing a different career path, or should I transfer to another branch as a means of establishing a whole new set of goals?

After researching my options, I found that I would not be able to move from the enlisted ranks to the warrant officer ranks in the Navy until I became a Chief Petty Officer (equivalent to an E-7 in the Army and Marines). God opened up a new door through a conversation with a retired senior chief.

"Mike, you should consider Warrant Officer School in the Army," suggested the retired senior chief at HC-4, who was now a support contractor.

"Why that route, Chief?"

I had already changed branches once. It wasn't a different uniform I was after. Even more than becoming an officer, I desired greater learning opportunities bringing with it greater career challenges and upward mobility. I needed the stimulation and sense of movement. I never did well standing still. If I transferred to the Army or back to the Marine Corps I would be able to apply for Warrant Officer School from my existing rank.

"From what I see, Mike, you've got all the blocks checked for Army Warrant Officer School," the retired senior chief explained. "You've got the education, rank, and job experience. If I were you, I would send my packet in for review. I think they'd pick you up pretty quickly. I've got a friend in Officer Assignments. I'll give him a call and ask how your credentials would fare in the Army."

It wasn't long after my conversation with the retired chief that I sent my packet off for review and was selected for Army Warrant Officer School. I knew from past experience that an intra-service transfer doesn't materialize overnight. It would end up taking several months to make the transition from the Navy to the Army. When it finally happened, I found myself traveling to Dothan, Alabama.

Transitioning from the Navy to the Army in terms of paperwork, uniforms, and a change of location, I fully understood how military customs as well as designation of ranks were different in various branches. I was familiar with many of the variances, but for several months after transferring it was the smaller subtleties that kept tripping me up.

"Get down and give me some pushups, Candidate Dean. Or should I say, 'get on the deck'?" the officer in charge asked sarcastically.

"Yes, sir," I answered as I put my seabag aside and began doing pushups.

"Candidate Dean, you might as well take your 'seabag' and swim back to your boat! You'll never make it in the Army!"

I had already drawn undue attention to myself by using terms like "seabag" instead of duffle bag, and the "head" for what the Army calls the latrine. Though I had to endure some humiliation, I quickly made the necessary adjustments. And so, I would not be swimming back to my ship, but instead I would be heading to Fort Lee, Virginia, after completing my officer candidate training at Dothan.

The Warrant Officer program I was selected for was Aviation Maintenance. Obviously they placed me in that particular program because of my prior experience and training. However, I discovered I didn't need the FAA airframe and power plant license in the warrant officer program, but I would also discover down the road how that license played an important role in a future assignment. After completing Army WOCS, I was commissioned as a warrant officer one, but my rank was not made permanent until I successfully passed the second portion of my training at Fort Lee, the home of the Maintenance Officer and Test Pilot Aviation Courses. After graduating from the program at Fort Lee I was assigned to the First Calvary Division at Fort Hood, Texas.

At Fort Hood I was put in charge of maintenance for a UH-1H helicopter unit. Army personnel affectionately referred to these old iron birds as "Hueys." They are the Timex of Army helicopters—they "take a licking and keep on ticking." Hueys go all the way back to the early years of the Vietnam War where they were used heavily in many different types of missions, especially search-and-destroy. The first Hueys to operate in Vietnam were the Medevac HU-1s which arrived in April 1962, before the United States became officially involved in the conflict. These Hueys supported the South Vietnamese Army, but American crews flew them. In October of 1962, the first armed Hueys, equipped with 2.75-inch rockets and .30 caliber machine guns, began flying in Vietnam. The Huey "gunships" became escorts for Army and Marine transport helicopters. By the end of 1964, the Army was flying more than 300 A and B model Hueys!

During the next decade, the Huey was upgraded and modified based on lessons learned in combat. Bell Corporation introduced the

UH-1D and UH-1H variants. It was in Vietnam that Army and Marine soldiers first tested the new tactics of airmobile warfare. In a typical air assault mission, Huey helicopters inserted infantry deep within enemy territory while Huey gunships, equipped with machine guns, rockets, and grenade launchers, often escorted the transports. Within minutes, helicopters could insert entire battalions into the heart of enemy territory. This provided air mobility into areas of difficult terrain, and is a tactic still used today when warranted.[20]

The Huey became a symbol of U.S. combat forces in Vietnam as millions of people worldwide watched it fly in TV news reports. At its peak in March of 1970, the U.S. military operated more than 3,900 helicopters in the war in Vietnam and two-thirds of them were Hueys. Their impact was profound, not only in the new tactics and strategies of airmobile operations, but on the survival rate of battlefield casualties. U.S. Army patients made up 390,000 of the total number of people transported by Medevac (Huey) helicopters in Southeast Asia. Almost a third of this total (120,000) were combat casualties. The Huey airlifted ninety percent of these casualties directly to medical facilities.[21]

I was proud to be a part of the 1st Calvary Division, and I was even more amazed at the timing of events in my life and where these decisions were taking me. Some attribute such things to coincidence, luck, or fate. Yet, I have discovered over and over that God has the ultimate plan, and if we trust Him and follow the leading He places in our hearts, it will get us where He desires. There was no mistaking how each place the Lord had taken me was a building block for the next step. Looking back I see how the timing of becoming a helicopter maintenance officer with direct oversight of a helicopter unit was not only another piece of the bigger picture, but it also led directly toward some of the greatest challenges of my life.

7

DESERT SHIELD / DESERT STORM

A real man will never let his fear of death overpower his honor, his sense of duty to his country, and his innate manhood. Battle is the most magnificent competition in which a human being can indulge. It brings out all that is best and it removes all that is base.[22]

—*General George Patton*

"Incoming!" the pilot shouted.

We were conducting a test flight in a Huey UH-1H near the southern border of Iraq and the northern border of Saudi Arabia. A scud missile soared in front of our helicopter missing us by less than a hundred feet! The flash of a missile coming so close not only tweaked my adrenaline, but it made my stomach and other parts of my body eruct.

Operation Desert Storm was my first experience in combat, and this particular incident was my initiation to war. The scud landed on a gas station near a small border town causing an enormous explosion. We weren't even flying in an immediate attack area. Chances are, and given the way the Iraqi troops operated, it was either a random scud launch or a launch that went severely off course.

A soldier's first experience of being fired upon or coming close to death is both stimulating and frightening. In those moments there's no time to ponder the vast amounts of minutia attached to the discussions of whether wars are necessary or simply man's most despicable behavior on display. Italian political theorist Niccolò Machiavelli argued, "You should never let things get out of hand in order to avoid war. There is no avoiding war; it can only be postponed to the advantage of others." Machiavelli's statement came to life in 1990 when Iraqi dictator Saddam Hussein rose up and decided to seize hundreds of oil wells in Kuwait. The United Nations told Hussein to get out; however, he continued to occupy Kuwait from August through December of 1990. My unit was deployed in the fall of 1990 in preparation in case Hussein continued to ignore the UN's warnings.

In January of 1991, after numerous warnings, the United States and the UN gave a final ultimatum to Hussein which he ignored. Subsequently, the U.S. and the UN formulated a plan to force Iraq out of Kuwait. The Persian Gulf War began on 16 January, 1991. Hussein's armies left Kuwait in a mad tirade while setting 730 of the world's richest oil wells on fire. It was the worst fire in history! Those dealing with the fires said that without modern technology it would have taken 1,000 years for the oil wells to burn out. One person witnessing the oil well fires said that it was a hellish sight. At any moment this witness expected little demons to come running out of the fires.[23]

General H. Norman Schwarzkopf, USA Commander-in-Chief, U.S. Central Command, said in a message to the command on 16 January 1991:

Soldiers, sailors, airmen and Marines of the United States Central Command, this morning at 0300, we launched Operation Desert Storm, an offensive campaign that will enforce the United Nation's resolutions that Iraq must cease its rape and pillage of its weaker neighbor and withdraw its forces from Kuwait. My confidence in you is total. Our cause is just! Now you must be the thunder and lightning of Desert Storm. May God be with you, your loved ones at home, and our Country.

The following day, a multinational invasion of Kuwait began, led by the United States. Operation Desert Storm began with a coordinated attack which included Tomahawk land attack missiles (TLAMs) launched from U.S. cruisers, destroyers, and battleships in the Persian Gulf and Red Sea. The initial barrage of over 100 TLAMs took out heavily defended targets in the vicinity of Baghdad and made a critical contribution to eliminating Iraqi air defenses and command and control capabilities. Hundreds of combat aircraft and bombers from nine different nations attacked targets in and around Kuwait and Iraq. More than 4,000 bombing runs were flown by allied aircraft in the first week, and the pace continued for another four weeks before a ground invasion began.

Immediately after the beginning of allied bombing, Iraq launched scud missile attacks on Tel Aviv and Jerusalem. President George H.W. Bush worked hard to prevent Israel from taking its own action against Iraq. If Bush had been unable to persuade Israel not to attack, Arab countries might have deserted the coalition. During the war the United States used dozens of new weapons that had been developed and acquired during the ten-year-old Reagan-Bush military buildup. They included the air and sea-launched cruise missile, and a slow-flying unmanned rocket which read Iraqi terrain in order to fly at treetop level toward its targets.

Now, less than six months after completing Warrant Officer Training, I was part of the Persian Gulf War. I was not only in charge of maintenance for a 1st Calvary helicopter unit (E-227), I was also the officer in charge of the unit's movement. My adjustment from the Navy to Army life came as quickly as my transition from the enlisted ranks to officer status. I was back to sea as an Army officer in charge of a unit of helicopters being transported to the Persian Gulf. As the movements officer I supervised the loading and the unloading of the Hueys from ship to shore.

We were about to engage in a new kind of war. A war where technology led, and ground troops followed. Offshore firepower in the form of missiles with computerized directional devices gave them near pinpoint accuracy. This opening barrage of missiles visited destruction upon the enemy, driving them into bunkers and keeping them hidden or on the move until the barrage was over. Afterward, air and ground forces would sweep in. And yet, even in the midst of the newest technology, many of the older and well-proven vehicles of war like the Huey were still needed. As military trucks delivered fuel on the ground, the reliable Hueys moved troops through the air and evacuated casualties. The fact is, every unit and every branch of the military provided a necessary component of fighting and winning the war.

"Sirens! Gas, gas, gas! Get your masks on . . . get your masks on!"

We were stationed near the Iraqi border just inside the war zone. The Iraqi Army was launching scud missiles armed with chemicals. When our warning sirens went off alerting us of another scud missile attack, our first order was to don our gas masks. We all worked long hours. Sleep was usually welcomed, and many times deep. When you're awakened from a deep sleep, it's difficult to instantly stir your body and its senses. The siren prompted me to run from my tent to the enlisted soldiers' tent yelling at the top of my lungs, "Gas, gas, gas!"

Many of the enlisted men were young, and many were not career military. They came to war with knowledge of how Saddam Hussein had used chemical agents on many of his own people and killed thousands in neighboring countries through chemical attacks. Most of us were more concerned about chemical agents being unleashed on us than we were about being shot. As I ran into the enlisted tent, I caught a glimpse of the frightened faces staring at me with my chemical mask on while shouting at them to don theirs. We survived the scud attack that night, but knew another one could come at any time.

After seeing the frightened faces of young warriors, I realized how death in war is a sad but unavoidable certainty. No matter how much we train, no matter how prepared we are, someone, somewhere, at some time will die. In reality, war has been with us since Cain killed Abel. As long as evil exists, there will be envy, hatred, and strife. Solomon expressed it as only he could: "Wisdom is better than weapons of war; but one sinner destroys much good."[24] Consequently, there remained a sorrowful certainty in my heart toward the soldiers I was surrounded by—I knew that good men and women would die, and loved ones would be left with hearts longing for the voices of those who had gone to the grave. This caused me to look inwardly. Was I ready? The conclusion I came to was that a man cannot fight if he is afraid of death.

There are many things I remember about war. Sometimes the most distinct memories are not of the explosions or chaos around you. There is another casualty of war which is often forgotten. This particular source of heartache can occur during peacetime, during prewar deployment, and in the theater of operation. Its effects can sometimes lead to an untimely death, but so often it results in an ongoing burden deep within one's soul. The source of this pain was given a name many wars ago—it's the "Dear John" letter.

Anyone who has been in the military, and far away from their family, understands the loneliness and the constant longing to be back in the arms of the ones they love. Many times the only things keeping a soldier going are his devotion to duty, his commitment to those whom he's fighting alongside, and his memories of the ones he desires to see if he's fortunate enough to return home.

During Desert Shield I often found myself helping other soldiers through the day, or through the stillness of the desert nights as I listened to them talk about their families and how they dreamed of seeing them again. I also wondered how life was at home. I often thought of my family and how it would be to see them face-to-face. Yet, there is a strong sense of responsibility that comes with command, and an innate desire to be strong for the sake of those serving under you.

"How are things at home?" I asked a young specialist named Daniel, who had been married less than six months.

He didn't answer.

As he sat staring into the vast darkness of the cool desert night, I saw him reach into his pocket and pull out a letter. "Oh no," I thought to myself, "another casualty!" It was beyond my comprehension how anyone could send a Dear John letter to someone who is thousands of miles away in a war zone. While it is certainly true that a soldier's family members back home suffer hardship in many ways, there seems to be a certain degree of coldheartedness, and even cowardice, in sending a Dear John letter to a soldier at war. It would seem more honorable for those in a relatively safe environment back home (despite their difficulties) to somehow muster the courage to wait and speak face-to-face with the loved one they kissed and sent off to war while promising to be faithful.

"It's a letter from my wife, Mr. Dean," Daniel said as he unfolded the paper. "She says she doesn't love me anymore."

This brave young soldier began cry. He looked at me with tears running down his dust-covered face. I was trained to lead, to fight, and to solve problems all along the way. However, at times like these I felt completely ill-equipped. WOCS cannot prepare an officer for this type of duty. I couldn't solve his problem. I didn't have just the right words to make everything okay and then get him focused back on the task at hand. What a helpless feeling for a man who had supervised the transportation of a squadron of helicopters to the Gulf, who was in charge of overseeing the maintenance and readiness of the unit. I had no military manual for fixing a broken heart. Now, it wasn't just foreign soil he was fighting on; he now had a tremendous battle within himself.

Daniel was overwhelmed. I put my hand on his shoulder and said, "We'll get through this together."

After saying a prayer for him, we sat and talked for quite some time.

This news nearly devastated him on top of what he had been through prior to our deployment. I got to know Daniel shortly after arriving at Fort Hood. When the news of our deployment to the Gulf was made known, our lives were suddenly shifted into high gear. Predeployment operations are not only hectic, but we also had to make sure everything was in order in our personal lives. We were forced to ask ourselves many questions. What if I don't return home? Will my family be taken care of? Are there bills needing to be paid? Are my insurance and will up-to-date? After hearing the news of deployment, Daniel quickly married his girlfriend to make sure she would be taken care of in case anything happened to him.

Daniel's world was shaken to the core even before leaving for the Gulf. While he was attempting to get his life organized and ready for deployment, his closest friend invited his mother down to see him before his departure. His friend's mother arrived and visited for a few days. Daniel's buddy Frank, who was also a soldier in my platoon, always had a cheerful disposition and was a friend to everyone. As his mother was flying out, Frank went to a hotel room, sat on the edge of the bed, put the barrel of a rifle in his mouth and killed himself.

One thing leaders discover very quickly: Leadership requires putting others first. Those who have never been in leadership sometimes don't understand the double-edged sword of commitment. They must be committed to their own family as well as to their military family. This task is never easy, and inevitably somebody is going to get shortchanged. Even though there were days I questioned myself, wondering about my own resolve, I always felt a strong sense of devotion to both.

I became a little flush as I heard Daniel say, "Maybe I should handle this like Frank did."

"That's not the answer," I said quickly. "You've got a lot to live for!"

My heart goes out to all the Daniels who have endured such heartache on the front lines of war. I kept an eye on him because I didn't want him getting so depressed he would even consider taking his own life. I was convinced we could make it through together just as so many soldiers have done in the past.

"Rapid dominance" is a military doctrine based on the use of overwhelming power, dominant battlefield awareness, dominant maneuvers, and spectacular displays of force to paralyze an adversary's perception of the battlefield and destroy its will to fight. Another name for this military tactic is "shock and awe," though it wasn't analyzed as such and given a name until 1996 at the National Defense University of the United States.

Rapid dominance was the initial method of invasion during Desert Shield/Desert Storm. Under the command of General Schwarzkopf, the Iraqi troops were pummeled by missiles from offshore as well as an extensive aircraft campaign before troops began to move from Saudi Arabia into Iraq.

The air war consisted of Navy and Marine Corps pilots and aircrews, and was the most powerful and successful air assault in the history of modern warfare. From "H-hour" on 17 January when the air campaign began, until the end of offensive combat operations forty-three days later, Navy and Marine aviators destroyed key targets and helped ensure that the United States military and its coalition partners owned the skies over Iraq and Kuwait.

The air campaign operated from six aircraft carriers, two large amphibious assault ships, a variety of other amphibious ships, plus ground bases and makeshift airstrips ashore. Navy and Marine fixed-wing and rotary-wing aircraft were an integral part of the coalition air campaign. Of more than 94,000 sorties flown by U.S. aircraft during the war, Navy and Marine aircraft flew close to 30,000. Sea-service pilots flew around 35 percent of the sorties, which was in direct proportion to their numbers in the U.S. air inventory. More than 1,000 Navy and Marine Corps aircraft joined the U.S. Air Force and Army coalition partners to knock out the Iraqi military machine. The air campaign was conducted in four phases. Phase I was to gain air superiority by destroying Iraq's strategic capabilities. That phase was accomplished within the first seven days!

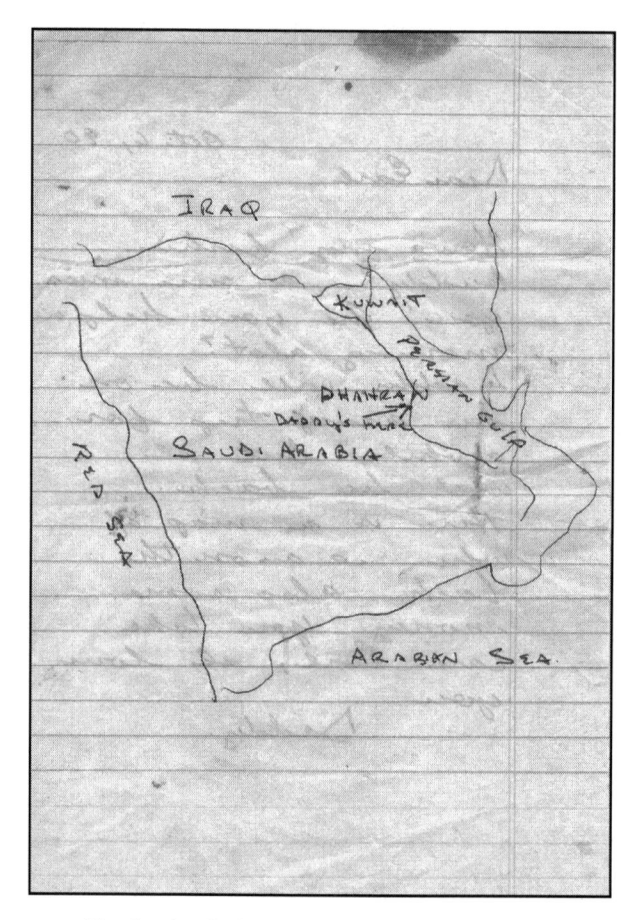

The back of a letter I sent to my young son
explaining where I was at in Iraq.

When my unit was given the order to advance into Iraqi territory, we saw firsthand the effects of General Schwarzkopf's air campaign. Twenty-five Hueys flew in formation over the Iraqi border, and it wasn't long before we began to see the destruction. We were short gunners for the .50 caliber machine guns so I took a gunner post as we flew in. A company of Hueys emerging out of the waves of desert heat was an amazing sight. To the surviving Iraqi troops, the formation of helicopters must have looked like a scene from *Apocalypse Now*.

As I looked down I could see that all that was left of many of the Republican Guard's tank battalions were smoldering masses of metal, charred bodies of soldiers who had tried to escape the burning tanks, and the remaining soldiers waving white flags of surrender. They were stuck in the middle of the desert with no supplies, injured soldiers, and no way of getting help. Five helicopters broke off and landed, surrounding a group of surrendering Iraqis.

Our unit continued to advance further into Iraq to provide eyes and cover for support companies on the ground. The U.S. military already had troops advanced well into the country that needed fuel and supplies. As we encountered other Iraqi troops (most of which were also surrendering due to the initial devastating attacks), we also landed and checked small villages. The only thing left in one small village was the rubble of what used to be stone houses, and one goat. Much of the destruction to the enemy's troops and vehicles was so fresh we could hear the moans of the injured and see the smoldering metal of bombed military vehicles.

There is much more I could say about fighting in a war. However, many books have already been written on this subject wherein a plethora of war stories have already been told. As I pen some of my own experiences, I discover the difficulty in discerning where the line is between being too sensational and simply describing it as it was. Yet, after a while all of the memories seem to mesh together in one large heap of painful wounds, burning flesh, destroyed property, and lives forever altered because of mankind's unbridled hatred and lust for power.

What I know of war is as personal to me as it is to any soldier. We each carry our own visions and we each have our own scars. When I think back, I see the faces of men and women too young to be enduring such hardships, but like so many before them they were forced to grow up quickly. I also see how God allows evil men to commit horrible atrocities, while at the same time I take comfort in knowing that one day we will all stand before our Maker and be judged accordingly.

For those I served with in Iraq, going home from war was an exhilarating time. We were provided an exceptional homecoming at Ft. Hood. Not only did families turn out to welcome us home, but also many from the community and even some from organizations who provide support for military families. Crowds lined the streets. People waved flags and cheered as our military caravan drove to a gymnasium on base. Crowds of cheering people and families packed the gymnasium. It was a true hero's welcome as families and friends reunited with loved ones coming home from war.

As exciting as it was to see my wife and kids, I noticed a man standing near us who seemed to be there by himself. He was older than me and wore a ball cap signifying he was a Vietnam veteran. I figured he might be a veteran who showed up to support the troops coming home from Iraq. Knowing how most Vietnam vets were met only with protests and hatred when they returned from war, I went over to speak to the gentleman.

"Thank you for coming here today," I said as I shook his hand. "And, welcome home."

It was an emotional moment. As much as I was enjoying the cheering crowds and reuniting with my wife and kids, I felt that this Vietnam veteran needed a "welcome home" even more than I.

"Thank you so much," he replied with tears in his eyes.

I could feel myself getting choked up as he knelt and hugged my kids. Every veteran needs to know they are appreciated, and all those returning from war deserve a proper welcome home.

Shortly after returning home I was awarded the Bronze Star for my service in Iraq. The Bronze Star is the fourth-highest combat decoration.

It is an individual military award of the United States Armed Forces, and may be awarded for heroism, acts of merit, or meritorious service in a combat zone. The citation reads as follows:

> To Warrant Officer Michael J. Dean for exceptionally meritorious service while serving as Allied Shops Section Leader, Echo Company, 227th Aviation Regiment, 1st Calvary Division during the period October 1990 to April 1991. Warrant Officer Dean's significant accomplishments contributed greatly to the outstanding success of the First Calvary Division during Operations Desert Shield and Desert Storm in Saudi Arabia, Iraq, and Kuwait. His actions have brought distinct credit upon himself, the First Calvary Division and the United States Army.

THE UNITED STATES OF AMERICA

TO ALL WHO SHALL SEE THESE PRESENTS, GREETING: THIS IS TO CERTIFY THAT THE PRESIDENT OF THE UNITED STATES OF AMERICA AUTHORIZED BY EXECUTIVE ORDER, 24 AUGUST 1962 HAS AWARDED

THE BRONZE STAR MEDAL

TO Warrant Officer Michael J. Dean

FOR Exceptionally meritorious service while serving as Allied Shops Section Leader, Echo Company, 227th Aviation Regiment, 1st Cavalry Division during the period October 1990 to April 1991. Warrant Officer Dean's significant accomplishments contributed greatly to the outstanding success of the First Cavalry Division during Operations Desert Shield and Desert Storm in Saudi Arabia, Iraq, and Kuwait. His actions have brought distinct credit upon himself, the First Cavalry Division and the United States Army.

GIVEN UNDER MY HAND IN THE CITY OF WASHINGTON
THIS 1st DAY OF April 1991

JOHN H. TILELLI JR.
Major General, U.S. Army
Commanding

8

HONDURAS

Within this shrine there lives the spirit of brotherhood binding the people of the United States with the nations of the world.

—*Indiana War Memorial*

After Desert Shield/Desert Storm I transferred from the 1st Calvary Division to the 504th Brigade, 15th Military Intelligence Battalion based out of Fort Hood, Texas. As part of my initial service in Military Intelligence, I agreed to take a one year unaccompanied tour in Honduras in exchange for going to school full time for two semesters in order to finish my undergraduate degree. The University of Central Texas was not far from Fort Hood. It was a great opportunity; however, the payback would mean being away from my family for an entire year.

My one year unaccompanied tour with the 15th MI was spent at Soto Cano Air Base (commonly known as Palmerola Air Base), which lies five miles to the south of Comayagua, Honduras. It is the home of five to six hundred U.S. troops, and it is also used by the Honduran Air Force Academy.

Soto Cano airbase became operational in 1981. The U.S. government once used Palmerola as a base of operations to support their foreign policy objectives in the 1980s. While I was stationed there, the U.S. military used Soto Cano as a launching point for its war on drugs in Central America as well as humanitarian aid missions throughout Honduras and Central America.

In addition to being the home of the Honduran Air Force Academy, the U.S. military's Joint Task Force Bravo (JTF-B) was also headquartered at Soto Cano. JTF-B consisted of a medical element (military hospital), Army forces, Air Force forces, joint security forces, and the 1st Battalion, 228th Aviation Regiment (consisting of some eighteen aircraft, a mix of UH-60 Black Hawk helicopters, and CH-47 Chinook helicopters).[25]

When I arrived at Soto Cano I felt as if I had stepped back in time. Most of the Honduran landscape was not only rural, but also Third World in its living conditions. The Miskito Indians were the largest native ethnic group in Honduras. I began my tour shortly after the Sandinistas were defeated in the elections, and the indigenous Miskitos had signed an agreement with the newly appointed minister of the interior to create "security zones" and prepare the return of the national police forces to the region with the goal of integrating fifty Miskito Indians into the police force. The U.S. military was still involved jointly with Honduran officials in a war against drugs, and Soto Cano was the hub of the joint activity.

On one occasion I had the opportunity to meet several Miskito Indians up close. During a mission that took us into the jungle, our Blackhawk helicopter began leaking hydraulic fluid. On board the helicopter were two pilots, three MI personnel, and two DEA agents. I listened in my headset as the pilots radioed Soto Cano telling them we were going to have to set the aircraft down in a clearing in the jungle. The return radio traffic explained how help would not be able to reach us until the morning. At night, the immensity of the nearby three-canopy jungle made a rescue operation undesirable. I didn't like the prospect of spending the night in the jungle, but I was thankful the pilots were able to land the helicopter safely.

There is something eerie about hearing jungle noises in the dead of night. Along with the humidity, the rustling of the trees, the cackling of birds and animals, and the unsettling feeling of not knowing who or what might be close by, I got a little taste of what our Vietnam heroes faced time and time again. As the sun came up, we came face-to-face with several Miskito Indians who stepped out into the clearing brandishing machetes. Thankfully, they were only curious about the noises they had been hearing during the night, and they turned out to be very friendly toward us. After help arrived, and the mechanics fixed the hydraulic leak, we were on our way.

Another memorable mission took place across the southern border of Honduras just inside of El Salvador. A U.S. Army major stationed at a consulate in El Salvador had been involved in a lover's triangle. Allowing his emotions to rule the day, he ended up killing the man who had been involved with his girlfriend. An El Salvadoran court ruled quickly, not allowing the U.S. military to take charge over their own personnel in order to try him under the UCMJ. With his execution scheduled, our unit had to act quickly. We flew into the city where he was being held and spent the night in a safe house. The next day we made our move and quickly extracted the major and then flew him back to Soto Cano.

Serving in Honduras offered many opportunities to be involved in intense drug interdiction operations—operations which I cannot speak about. While off duty, Soto Cano provided some incredible sightseeing tours made available by the military's recreation services.

A trip to Lake Yojoa was very memorable. This lake has a spectacular view. It has clear water, and, for a mountain lake, it has tremendous size and depth (up to forty meters deep). Its waters are also surprisingly warm. The altitude along the shore is about 600 meters. Surprisingly, Yojoa is best known for its bass which are stocked because they are not indigenous. Yojoa has become a sport fishing center. Some hotels along the lake even provide boats and water skiing.[26]

I used one of the unit's Jeeps to travel into the mountainous regions. However, I was always intrigued by how the locals traveled. Most were on foot. If they were fortunate enough to take a bus they would be subjected to many random stops at small villages for reasons buses in America would never agree to stop. For instance, a man in a small village might need to pick up a chicken from a friend to take home with him. You might even see livestock on the bus, or someone riding on the roof.

A lot of the villages along the road were full of huts like the ones I saw in Africa. I always took note of how content the children seemed to be, playing around the huts or the plain-looking stone houses. Their games might include a dirty old ball and a stick, and yet they seemed much happier than many American children who have all sorts of electronic gadgets, plenty of food, and more entertainment than kids in rural Honduras would ever dream possible.

An unaccompanied military tour can be very difficult for a soldier's family. Being physically away from your wife and kids, waiting for letters to arrive, not seeing your family on birthdays or at Christmas—it all weighs on you after a while. One of the keys for me to keep my mind from drifting into being too melancholy was to stay busy. The Honduran coast is the home of the world's second largest barrier reef where I spent time maintaining my scuba diving skills.

4th Battalion, 228th Aviation Regiment
Camp Pickett, Soto Cano Air Base, Honduras

HAPPY HOLIDAYS

WINGED WARRIORS
CHRISTMAS 1993

I also taught two semesters of Principles of Management at the airbase. This course was offered to military personnel through Central Texas College as a way to continue their education while on deployment. Like most colleges, it required instructors to have a graduate degree. However, the pool of qualified personnel was limited, and since I was working on my master's I was provided a waiver to teach.

I always tried to make the most of every assignment. In hindsight I could clearly see how my deployment to Honduras was another block checked in the bigger picture. I was glad when I returned to the States, but I was also glad that I had exchanged the tour for completing my undergraduate degree, which allowed me to continue to advance in rank. My advancement within the warrant officer ranks is eventually what opened the door to service in the Unit. These are all observations gained from hindsight.

9

15ᵀᴴ MI

"I once played golf with President Eisenhower. It's hard to play a guy who rattles his medals while you're putting."[27]

I saw Bob Hope for the second time in my life. He and his wife Deloris had stopped at Fort Hood on a book tour. His book, entitled *I Was There*, marked half a century of entertaining America's soldiers. A paragraph from his book, written after one of his World War II USO tours, explains why he had such a passion for giving something back to America's armed forces:

> The trip, the shows, the close calls had quite an effect on me. My priorities changed—I felt good about myself but realized that any contribution I was making was minimal. I was offering time and laughs—the men and women fighting the war were offering up their lives. Dedication to one's country took on a whole new meaning. I helped them laugh. They taught me what sacrifice was all about.[28]

Once in a while I stopped and reflected on my military journey. I began in the Marines, transferred to the Navy, then to the Army where I served in the 1st Calvary Division, and was now serving in Military Intelligence. I had no idea when I flew off to boot camp where I would end up over a decade later. The 15th Military Intelligence Battalion was within the 504th Military Intelligence Brigade. Its lineage can be traced all the way back to the 137th Signal Radio Intelligence Company activated in the early days of World War II. The 137th earned battle streamers for the campaigns of Northern France, Central Europe, and the Rhineland.

After World War II the brigade's name and tasks were subject to many changes. On 21 April 1978, the 504th Military Intelligence Group (Corps) was activated and began its evolution to a Military Intelligence Brigade. On 16 September 1985, the brigade was designated as the 504th Military Intelligence Brigade (Corps) at Fort Hood and supported the 3rd Armored Corps. At that time the brigade consisted of a Headquarters and Headquarters Detachment and three Military Intelligence Battalions: 15th Military Intelligence Battalion (Aerial Exploitation), the 163rd Military Intelligence Battalion (Tactical Exploitation), and the 303rd Military Intelligence Battalion (Operations).

To fulfill its new mission the brigade relinquished control of the 15th Military Intelligence Battalion and activated three new companies: a Network Support Company, a Forward Support Company, and a Long Range Surveillance Troop (B-38th CAV) while restructuring the Headquarters and Headquarters Detachment into a company expanding its missions. The two remaining Military Intelligence battalions assumed identical missions as intelligence collection battalions.[29]

After returning to Fort Hood, I continued in my duties as a maintenance officer, and also as a COR, or contracting officer's representative. This was necessary because we had civilian personnel doing maintenance on fixed-wing aircraft, and there had to be military representatives providing oversight. Up to this point in my career I had managed rotor units (helicopters), but the 15th MI put me in charge of fixed-wing maintenance as well as oversight of their UAVs (unmanned arial vehicles).

One of the most memorable deployments with the 15th MI was to Korea. During this deployment I was in charge of the support aircraft for our mission. We were working near the southern tip of Korea in the area of Pusan. I thought it was interesting how on this particular mission we had a Russian linguist attached to our unit. Intelligence units are always compartmentalized, and information is only provided on a need-to-know basis. One evening we decided to eat at a Russian restaurant where we met several Russian sailors who were crew members of a Russian three-mast sailing ship called the Pallada. The ship was used by the Russian Naval Academy as a training ship for team-building exercises. They were anchored for a port call.

After spending an evening talking with the Pallada's crew, the captain of the ship invited several from our unit aboard the ship. Our Russian linguist accompanied us, and onboard we met a Russian university professor who spoke fluent English. After talking with the crew below deck for several hours, the professor asked me to climb the center mast (about 100 feet high) into the crow's nest. I took him up on it. We both strapped on the necessary climbing gear for safety and made our way to the top. (I still have the climbing gear.)

As we enjoyed the view of the city lights and the harbor, we conversed until early morning. Much of our conversation had to do with the similarities and differences of our two cultures.

"You know Michael, Russian soldiers train hard just as you do."

"I'm sure that's true, Professor."

"They also love their families, and they love their country just as you do."

"I'm sure that's also true," I responded.

Having grown up in the 1960s and early 70s, I still remembered the Cold War with Russia. I could visualize the bomb drills we had in grade school to prepare for the possibility of a nuclear attack. In my wildest dreams, I never would have guessed that one day I would spend hours in the crow's nest of a Russian three-mast sailing ship with a Russian professor while watching the sunrise over the coast of South Korea! It was an extraordinary sunrise to boot.

At the end of our conversation, and as the sunrise was exploding in the eastern sky, the Russian professor put his hand on my shoulder and said, "Michael, my friend, you and I are not all that different."

Then the professor put both hands on my shoulders and looked me in the eyes. He moved in close, making sure we had eye contact and said in a very serious tone, "But always remember this, Michael . . . there's coming a day when the one you and I will have to watch will be China." The tone in his voice, and the sincerity with which he spoke, left me speechless. To this day, I often think about what he said and wonder about the implications.

Back at Fort Hood, my role within the 15th MI involved a lot of flight hours and constant oversight of maintenance operations. As it was with the majority of my career to this point, it was only in hindsight that I would understand how the culmination of my experiences would catch the attention of the Unit. Even while serving in the 15th MI, I was unaware that the Unit even existed. It wasn't on my radar, nor could it have been as a potential career move.

The next logical step for me was the Senior Warrant Officer course. As it is with any career, advancement is contingent upon continuing education and a willingness to accept more responsibility. I was always hungry to learn and enjoyed the demands of more being expected of me, because I expected a lot of myself. It challenged me to never be satisfied and to always be on my toes.

The Senior Warrant Officer course was instructive, and I was enjoying the classes and hands-on training. This course was a fulfillment of the requirement for my Chief Warrant Officer Three rank. The silver bar with three black squares on it was equivalent to the pay grade of an Army captain. At the time, there was only one more pay grade in the warrant officer ranks. I had almost gone as far as I could go in this current line of advancement, but I was feeling settled about where I was at. Little did I know I was approaching a significant turn in my military career—a turn that I couldn't have seen coming.

It was during my time at the SWO course that I was recruited by the Unit. Most people, even many military personnel, do not know the Unit exists or, if they are aware, they're not informed concerning its mission. I cannot expound upon their method of recruitment. Needless to say, when I was approached I agreed to climb aboard.

Within this book I have purposely been very brief in my descriptions of the Unit's operations. I have only spoken of that which is either already known (i.e. published) or does not in any way inhibit, jeopardize, or expose any unit members or their operations. I have far too great a respect for all those involved in the Unit, and I carry with me a sense of duty and honor I will never violate.

My military career came to a close while I was with the Unit. Upon my retirement I was awarded the Legion of Merit—a military award of the United States Armed Forces given for exceptionally meritorious conduct in the performance of outstanding services and achievements. It is the sixth highest in the order of precedence of the U.S. military awards.

Mike Dean

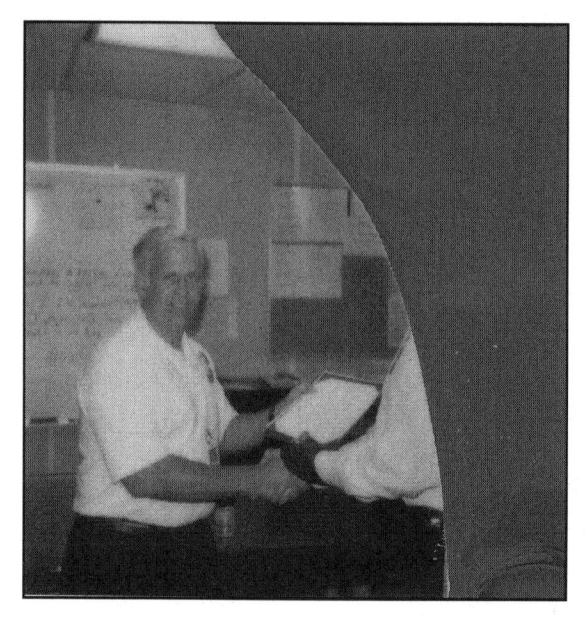

Receiving the Legion of Merit my last day with the Unit.

This award contained the following citation:

> For distinctly superior, highly meritorious service in a succession of increasingly challenging positions culminating in assignment to a unique Special Operations and Intelligence Unit. During his Military Service, Chief Warrant Officer Three Dean clearly distinguished himself through unwavering commitment to selfless performance, absolute dedication to the highest standards of performance and sincere caring for fellow Soldiers and Service Comrades. He has made a direct, meaningful contribution to Soldier, Unit and Army readiness at every duty station and in every capacity. He has set his subordinates, peers and superiors up for full mission success in every instance. Chief Warrant

Officer Three Dean's service legacy reflects his extreme pride in the collective accomplishment of Units and Teams he's been a part of, extraordinary patriotism and adherence to core Army values. Chief Warrant Officer Three Dean's singular Service Accomplishments are in the finest traditions of Military Service and reflect the utmost credit upon him, this Command and the United States Army.

Signed by:

Robert W. Noonan, Jr. Major General,
USA Commanding General and the Secretary of the Army.

I am very proud to have served with such a skilled, dedicated, and patriotic group of soldiers! For that matter, all of my military service was spent with some of the finest men and women America has to offer. I pray that America will continue to cultivate the proud tradition through which we protect and defend our Constitution and the citizens of our great nation.

10

FULL CIRCLE

Our birth is nothing but our death begun.[30]

Writing this book has caused me to count my blessings as I see God's providential hand during and even after the conclusion of my military career. As I reflect upon the full scope of my military service, I cannot help but consider the life of a close friend Colonel Jim Tirey. His life reminds me of how all of us should be extending a helping hand to others while taking every opportunity to express words of encouragement. Every life, whether successful or obscure, is somehow connected to others—even if it's only a few. Jim was one of those men whose life was connected to countless others because he was selfless in his service, undaunted in his devotion to duty, and most importantly, was loyal to his friends and family. He was the type of person you could count on to help you anytime and anywhere.

I will never forget standing beside Lt. General John F. Kimmons at Arlington National Cemetery as I watched Jim's horse-drawn caisson rolling through the sea of white headstones which mark the graves of thousands of soldiers who had gone on before him. Many thoughts traversed my mind as the caisson came to a stop at his grave site—the type of thoughts one has upon the death of someone so close. My world paused for a moment as I thought of Jim and how much influence his life had on so many others. This thought bore witness as I looked around and saw several hundred people from all walks of life—including a number of generals and high-ranking officials—who came to pay their final respects to a man who had lived such an honorable life. The crowd of people was a true conformation of the impact of the life of Jim Tirey.

A flag-draped coffin, hearing taps played at the graveside, and the sound of a twenty-one gun salute all represent the very emotional and solemn way in which a fellow soldier is laid to rest. The influence of Colonel Tirey's life was spoken of with great clarity by a general who knew him well. After the graveside service ended, and he was laid to rest among the seemingly unending rows of soldiers' graves, it was rather sad to imagine that those passing by in the future would only know Colonel Tirey by an inscription and two dates.

There are two days which are common to everyone—the day we're born and the day we die. However, the most important dates are all those in between. It is what we do on those days that we will be remembered for. Losing a friend or loved one tends to stir a sense of reflection. We might ask ourselves how we will be remembered. What will I do with my remaining time here on the earth? My career in the military had come to an end, but I still had many things left to accomplish.

After retiring from the military I went into the aviation business in Florida with two friends. Even in "retirement" I was continually amazed at some of the well-known and well-connected individuals whose paths crossed with mine. I attribute this to the providential occurrences which can happen in any individual's life as they make use of their God-given gifts. For instance, on one occasion I was asked by the office of

Governor Jeb Bush to be part of a Trade Commission delegation to Chile and Argentina. Not only was it exciting to travel with Governor Bush and his wife, but while on the trip I was privileged to meet the president of Argentina.

On another occasion, and while doing work for a Canadian aircraft company, I traveled to the Paris Air Show to assist them in the marketing of an aircraft we had completed integration and modifications on. While in Paris I was invited to the Canadian ambassador's house where I met several dignitaries, astronauts, and entertainers.

After leaving the business in Florida, I was offered a position as a contractor supporting the U.S. Army Intelligence Security Command in Washington, D.C. From there I went on to the Pentagon to support the Army's Counter IED Task Force. After spending some time in the Beltway, it began to take its toll. I decided to move back home to Indiana after being offered a position with the Department of Defense, which also satisfied a desire I had to get back to my roots.

I often think back to my teenage years as I looked out the window of a high school classroom dreaming of ocean surfs, mountain peaks, foreign lands, and living on the edge of danger. During the spring of 2012 I looked out the window of a privately chartered flight from Anchorage to Anvik, Alaska, and thought about how my life had come full circle. I reminisced about the small town I grew up in and the small town I currently lived in. I pictured my wife and thought about how our reuniting was the passion and peak of my life's story. All of my adventures notwithstanding, it's when I reunited with her that my life truly became complete.

Undoubtedly, there's great satisfaction in fulfilling your dreams. Solomon said in Proverbs 13:19, "A desire accomplished is sweet to the soul." I've discovered how even when you think you've accomplished all you've ever desired to do, there may be one more thing. A man should never stop dreaming. I've also discovered how an adventurous soul may never be satisfied. A "bucket list" consists of the top desires one would like to accomplish before they die, or before they "kick the bucket." Like many people, I too have a bucket list. Though I will admit my bucket is pretty full, there are still a few things that remain.

As I flew over the Alaskan landscape I found myself spellbound by its beauty. The treetops, lakes, and mountainous regions were even more breathtaking than I had imagined. I was in the midst of experiencing one of the top items on my bucket list—a trip to Anvik River Lodge. Having to book the trip two years in advance created enormous anticipation! As I traveled 450 miles by air into the interior of Alaska, I was on the brink of another adventure. I was intent on enjoying every moment. There were seven others on the plane who had also waited for their turn to travel to Anvik.

While in the air I thought of Alaskan aviator Jack Jeffords, a pioneer in the Alaskan frontier who lived on the edge every time he climbed into his plane. Being a pilot myself, I appreciated the skill and grit it would take to do what Jeffords did flying rescue missions, delivering mail, and helping to settle the Alaskan frontier in the 1930s. In three short years he became the chief pilot of the CAA, forerunner of the FAA, as he hunted coyotes, counted reindeer, and transported prisoners and congressmen.

After landing on a small airstrip, our journey began with a comfortable boat ride from the shores of the Yukon River up the Anvik River to the lodge. The Anvik Lodge was everything one might expect, and very accommodating. We didn't see other fishing tours, boaters, or float planes during our stay. It was just eight guests, the Anvik River Lodge staff, and the wildlife on 120 miles of river which is a tributary of the Yukon River. Our nearest neighbor was about seventy miles downstream in the Athabascan village of Anvik—a small village pioneered by missionaries.

At the lodge we discovered all the comforts of home, yet in a very remote setting. The hand-hewn main lodge housed ten to twelve guests in five rooms, each with private baths. The rooms opened out onto the hub of the lodge's activity—a massive great room with a vaulted ceiling and a picture window. This is where we enjoyed dining and socializing around fabulous meals and conversations about the magnificent scenery and amazing surroundings. The food at the Anvik Lodge was topnotch. They served traditional food along with vegetables grown in their own garden. Homemade bread along with cookies and desserts all accompanied the hearty meals. The lodge is also well-known for its steak and king crab extravaganzas.

The river was clear as glass. It was the same river used as a trade route for Russian explorers on their way to the mighty Yukon. I spent my time in Anvik fishing for Pacific salmon, northern pike, arctic char, Dolly Varden, arctic grayling, and whitefish. I could look down at the river and see massive schools of fish. I caught so many fish my first day I thought my arm would give out. We were told that wildlife sightings may include moose, gray and black wolves, otters, beavers, eagles, ospreys, and over fifty other species of migratory and songbirds that make their home in Anvik. However, one grizzly bear sighting was unexpected and also frightening.

Our guide steered our fishing boat to the shore in order to clean and cook some fish. As we chatted by the riverside, a large moose and her calf came running out of the woods. They jumped frantically into the river and began to swim to the other side. Moments later a grizzly bear ran out of the woods directly toward our picnic site. The two guides yelled for us to get back into the boat as they began to shoot at the feet of the bear. The guides knew that bears have very poor eyesight, and they either saw us as food or a threat. Our guides wanted to make sure the bear understood us as a threat. When the bear stood up on its hind legs and growled, the guides laid down another string of fire at its feet. After the second round of gunfire, the grizzly swatted at the ground with one of its enormous front paws, and ran back into the woods.

A beautiful spot for a cookout on the shore of the Anvik River.

After fly-fishing for salmon, I thought about the life cycle of this fascinating and very tasty species. A salmon's primary effort is to fight their way upstream only to spawn and then die. This may well personify the efforts of so many people in the course of their lives.

How sad it is if we do not make an effort to pursue our dreams. If death is within us from the moment we are born, then it becomes our duty before God to do everything He has called and gifted us to do. Then, as our lives progress, and one day as we're looking back, we can see a full circle. Each of us has a story either in the process of being written, or waiting to be written. I leave you with the pages of this book that have no eyes, only words meant to inspire . . .

"A soldier's story . . ."

EPILOGUE

A HISTORY OF SUCCESS THROUGH PERSEVERANCE

I speak of a time within the memory of men now living. I speak of a time within the memory of some who hear me. These will bear witness to the truth of what I say.
—William Wesley Woolen, 1883

Sir Francis Bacon said, "Histories make men wise; poets witty; the mathematics subtle; natural philosophy deep; moral grave; logic and rhetoric able to contend." In biblical times, the history of families and nations had deep significance. Job 8:8-10 is instructive: "For inquire, please, of the former age, and consider the things discovered by their fathers; for we were born yesterday, and know nothing, because our days on earth are a shadow. Will they not teach you and tell you, and utter words from their heart?"

The treasure of history is found in the study of how one person's life, though comparatively insignificant, can impact so many others. Its sustenance lies in the lessons learned from our forefathers who persevered and set examples for us to follow. The brightest colors woven on history's tapestry are those which teach us how to overcome trials and serve others in such a way as to elevate their lives to great heights of human accomplishment while, in the process, giving glory to our Maker.

In the introduction I mentioned my great-aunt who was born two years before Lincoln's assassination. This particular aunt was one of the first women to graduate from Franklin College in 1895. She became a professor, and later became a chiropractor and operated a practice in Indianapolis. The pleasant reminiscing this book has required has also led me to uncover another truly American story beginning at a time before the Revolutionary War. A story of three brothers who, while exercising great courage, found an "abundance of food for philosophical reflection."[31] Men who spent their childhoods working on a farm in Maryland and later became the president of a bank, a physician and state senator, and the attorney general of the state of Indiana. I offer you this story with the same intentions their parents had—"to engraft upon the minds of their children such principles as would ensure a life of honor and usefulness."[32]

In the forepart of the seventeenth century, the Woollen family emigrated from London to America. On the voyage the father and all the children died of disease which was typical of many of these journeys. Mrs. Woollen, who was pregnant, was the lone survivor amongst her family. After reaching Philadelphia, she gave birth to a son she named John from whom sprang all of the Woollens now known to be in this country.[33]

In 1642, about 180 years before Indiana statehood, Captain George Lamberton led an English colony from New Haven into Delaware. In his employ was an Indian interpreter named John Woollen. After drifting down the peninsula to the eastern shore of Maryland, he took up residence in an English settlement on Taylor's Island in the Chesapeake Bay. It was there that John Woollen had a son named William who was the grandfather of three brothers named William, Thomas, and Levin Woollen.

Those were the days when the New World was up for grabs. Only a few years earlier (1638) the region had been established as a Swedish colony and included parts of present-day Pennsylvania, New Jersey, and Delaware.[34] Lamberton and Woollen soon ran into trouble. In 1643 Johan Bjornsson Printz was appointed governor of the Swedish Colony of New Sweden. Printz succeeded in expelling the English who had settled under Lamberton. He attacked them, burned down their trading-house, and put Lamberton in irons.

As the story goes, Lamberton was in his pinnace (a small sailing boat) anchored about three miles above Fort Elfsberg, located on the New Jersey side of the Delaware River, between present-day Salem and Alloway Creek. Two Swedes arrived with a letter from Governor Printz purporting that the Indians had stolen a gold chain from his wife, and those Indians had been trading with Lamberton the same day as the theft. He asked that Lamberton stay aboard his vessel until the next day so he could identify the Indians who had stolen the gold chain. The next day there were no visitors. It is said that Lamberton received another letter from the governor requesting he make an appearance at the Swedish fort. Knowing that he had done nothing wrong, Lamberton willingly went to see the governor.

Upon his arrival, Printz ordered that Lamberton be arrested. In his company was his Indian interpreter, John Woollen, who was also put in irons. In *Sketches of Three Brothers*, the following is recorded about the integrity Woollen exhibited throughout this situation:

It is asserted that Printz's wife and Timothy, the barber (surgeon), endeavored to get Woollen intoxicated by giving him a quantity of wine and beer to drink, and that, immediately after drinking the liquors, he was conveyed to Printz, who, "with professions of a great deal of love to him, making him many large promises to do him good," endeavored to get him to say "that George Lamberton had hired the Indians to cut off the Swedes." Woollen denied that Lamberton had any such intention. The Governor then "drunk to him again," and said he would make him a man, give him a plantation, and build him a house, and that he should not want for gold and silver, provided he made the accusation against Lamberton. But, Woollen still refusing to accuse Lamberton, the Governor was much enraged, and stamped his feet, and, calling for irons, "he put them upon Woollen with his own hands, and sent him down to prison."[35]

It was written of John Woollen that "he resisted the two greatest temptations of mankind; namely, wine and money. It can truthfully be said of his descendants that no one of them ever proved false to a friend or sacrificed his manhood for money."[36] Old John Woollen (as he was called) is also written about in Vincent's *History of Delaware*. The historian of Delaware described him as a man who "transmitted his integrity to his descendants."

Cultural legacies are powerful forces. They have deep roots and long lives. They persist, generation after generation, virtually intact, even as the economic and social and demographic conditions that spawned them have vanished, and they play such a role in directing attitudes and behavior that we cannot make sense of our world without them.

—Malcomb Gladwell, *Outliers: The Story of Success*

In 1820, a location in the center of the state of Indiana was selected for the capital city. Jeremiah Sullivan, a justice of the Indiana Supreme Court, came up with the name Indianapolis by joining *Indiana* with *polis*, the Greek word for city. Though not particularly clever, the name Indianapolis literally means "Indiana City." At the time, it was in the wild and sixty miles from the nearest settlement. It became the seat of the state government in 1825, just three years before the eldest brother of this story was born.

On June 21, 1828, William Wesley Woollen was born in Maryland to Edward and Anna (Wheeler) Woollen, twelve years after Indiana was admitted to the union. The year he was born, President John Quincy Adams was being challenged by Andrew Jackson who would become president in November of that year. The newly-formed Indiana government was rapidly taking shape, and proved to have big plans for transforming a tribal wilderness into a developed state with important populous centers. As the northern tribal lands gradually opened to white settlements, Indiana's population rapidly increased and shifted northward.

Two years later, on April 26, 1830, Thomas Wheeler Woollen was born; and four years after that, on June 30, 1834, Levin James Woollen was born. Their parents (Edward and Anna Woollen) were among the oldest families in the state of Maryland, being identified with its first settlement. All three brothers were born in Dorchester County,

Maryland, and all three had the privilege of working on the family farm as they grew into men.

Writing about the Woollen brothers in *Representative Men of Indiana*, the biographer states:

> The world is full of such examples, and the student of biography will have no difficulty in recalling instances in which farm life in youth left its indelible impress upon the most exalted characters known to history. In these early years, when the mind is taking its bent, when youthful ambitions are shaping themselves for manhood achievements, no influences have ever been found more potential for good than those which the farm has afforded. The frugalities of the farmer's home, the chaste purity of its teachings, the broad fields, the forests, the orchard and the meadow, hill and dell, the songs of the birds and the hum of bees, the laughing brook, the silent river—all the wealth of beauty that nature spreads out with a lavish hand—are the teachers of youth whose lessons are never forgotten.[37]

Life on the farm in the middle 1800s was not only isolated, but many rural Americans had limited transportation and had to rely upon their independent spirit and sense of ingenuity in order to succeed. For most, times were hard, days were long, and the rewards were minimal. One North Carolina newspaper, the *Fayetteville Observer*, in 1837, proudly pointed out: "The great mass of our population is composed of people who cultivate their own soil, owe no debt, and live within their means. It is true we have no overgrown fortunes, but it is also true that we have few beggars."[38]

Rural life gave the Woollen family a great sense of unity and created an atmosphere that fostered an impeccable work ethic. For William, farm life produced self-reliance, poise, and confidence in his own ability to overcome obstacles and achieve success. He desired to explore. This desire led him to the "Great West."

> For a youth of sixteen summers, without the patronage of friends, and with limited means, to take upon himself all the chances of failure or success in a strange land and among strangers, must be accepted as proof positive of the possession of those sturdy qualities of head and heart upon which communities and states rely for growth and renown.[39]

William Woollen arrived in Madison, Indiana, in December of 1844 with one dollar and seventy-five cents in his pocket. He remained a citizen of Indiana until his death. In his formative years he was, for the most part, self-educated, a voracious reader with a hunger for knowledge. Upon his arrival in Indiana he found employment as a schoolteacher, during which time his desire for higher education only increased. In the years that followed he attended Hanover College and worked in the recorder's office of Jefferson County while at the same time studying law. No time was wasted in pursuit of higher endeavors.

As his professional life developed, William worked as a county clerk and county auditor, was elected to the office of treasurer of Jefferson County, bought half interest in a newspaper, opened a banking house (which eventually merged with First National Bank), and was elected president of the Indianapolis Board of Trade. Concerning his dealings as a public official, one writer said: "No official career was ever more honorable, none freer from the taint of suspicion; and no man ever took into retirement a larger share of esteem of the people."

The life and careers of his brothers were also exceptional, possessing the same innate integrity while amassing a great amount of esteem from those they served. Thomas Woollen arrived in Indiana four years after his brother William. After studying law, he settled in Franklin, Indiana, where he opened a law office. In 1862 he was elected to the legislature from Johnson County. In 1868 he was elected judge of the Court of Common Pleas of his district. In 1872 he was again elected to the legislature, and in 1878 he was elected to the position of attorney general for the state of Indiana.

Levin Woollen also had to rely upon his own resources, and had to study at night while working for a canning business. In 1849 he moved to Madison and worked for his brother William in the newspaper business. Afterward he entered the law office of the judge-advocate-general of the United States as a student. However, the study of law didn't suit Levin, and he began to study medicine with one of the most talented physicians the West has ever known—Dr. William Davidson. In 1857 he graduated from medical school at the University of Louisville, and practiced medicine until his death. In 1878, Dr. Woollen was also elected to the state Senate and was one of the most active members with a deep interest in all matters concerning public welfare.

All three of the Woollen brothers are prime examples of how anyone who has the desire to succeed, and the motivation to do whatever it takes, can accomplish great things. Vision, perseverance, and a fervent desire to attain success are all necessary, and great accomplishments await those who will put to work all of these principles. Stories like the Woollens not only provide a brushstroke on history's canvas, but even more importantly they serve as an inspiration to the generations that follow.

As I conclude this portion I can imagine someone saying, "These are interesting stories of fine Americans, but why have you attached them to the story of your military career?" The reason I felt compelled to share them is: William W. and Levin J. Woollen were my great-great uncles, and their brother Thomas W. Woollen was my great-great grandfather. My life and my passion for success has been fed, and even set ablaze, by their stories. I believe we all have greatness in our past we can draw from to invigorate our present goals, add fuel to our dreams, and provide courage for the future.

Thomas W. Woollen

The Woollens were on the maternal side of my family, and proved themselves to be great men and influential citizens of Indiana. Oftentimes you can tell a lot about the character of the man by his associates. Proverbs 20:18-20 tells us, "Plans are established by counsel;

by wise counsel wage war. He who goes about as a talebearer reveals secrets; therefore do not associate with one who flatters with his lips. Whoever curses his father or his mother, his lamp will be put out in deep darkness."

As I was doing research for this portion of the book, I acquired some of William W. Woollen's handwritten notes—notes he was making for his book *Biographical and Historical Sketches of Early Indiana*. In this book he mentions a close friend, William McKee Dunn, who was commissioned a brigadier general by President Abraham Lincoln. Of Dunn he says:

> Dunn had a mind far ahead of that possessed by many whose portion in life led the people to regard them as great men. But if goodness; if honor; if truthfulness; if morality and great human sympathy go to make up the character of a great man, then McKee Dunn was truly great. Off all the public men with whom I have been intimately acquainted, no one has left such an affectionate impression on my mind as has the late General William McKee Dunn.[40]

On the paternal side of my family I discovered an interesting nugget as well—a letter from Orville Wright to my great-grandfather Dr. James H. Dean. My grandfather was a graduate of Hartsville College and had built up one of the largest dental practices in Franklin, Indiana. He had requested that Mr. Wright speak at an alumni reunion at Hartsville College. Although Wright had to decline, the letter contains some interesting family information about him.

> ORVILLE WRIGHT
> DAYTON, OHIO
>
> August 1, 1946.
>
> Dr. J. H. Dean,
> Greenwood, Indiana.
>
> Dear Doctor Dean:-
>
> I have your letter of July 27th inviting me to attend Hartsville College Alumni reunion August 15th. I regret I can not attend.
>
> My mother was a student at Hartsville in the 1850's, and my older brothers Reuchlin and Lorin in the early 80's.
>
> My father was pastor of the College (University it was then called) from the Fall of 1867 to June 1869, when he became editor of the Religious Telescope at Dayton. Father while pastor taught a class in Theology.
>
> I inclose an old circular advertising Hartsville, found among my father's letters, which may have some interest for you. Originally it was a folder, the third and fourth pages left blank for writing. I assume the circulars were given to the ministers of the denomination for their use in writing letters, and at the same time to advertise the college. Unfortunately I cut the letter part off some years ago, so that I now am unable to establish the exact date of the circular. I suspect the date was in the 1860's or early seventies.
>
> Sincerely yours,
>
> Thanks
> Orville Wright

If your family history is not a story of integrity, perseverance, and success, then I would propose you change that pattern and allow the Lord to write a new story for your children and your grandchildren. Of course, this means allowing God to be the Author, and humbly submitting to His plans while trusting His pen to write your story. My ancestors relied upon and testified of the Lord's providence at work in their lives. Because of God's favor and divine grace, these words became their legacy:

> In such lives there are no startling incidents, no eccentricities of character. Such men in their walk and conversation, in their ambitions and aspirations, seek the table-lands of life, where, if there are no dizzy elevations of thought and fancy, there are, as a compensation, no depressions of infidelity and deceit. They in an atmosphere free from the malaria which breeds intellectual distempers, and, pursuing the even tenor of their ways, are to society what the fixed stars are to navigators. To such men as William Wesley Woollen society is largely indebted, not only for material progress, but for those ideas of order and security which form its chief guarantees of prosperity and progress.[41]

May we strive so that such words will be spoken of us, and then passed on to future generations!

APPENDIX
WISH FOR OUR HEROES

www.wishforourheroes.org

All of the proceeds from this book will be donated to WISH for OUR HEROES, a national 501(c)(3) dedicated to assisting the men and women of the United States active duty military. WISH for OUR HEROES was launched in November of 2009, in honor of 1SG Thomas G. Wells, who was a career Marine. The founders of WISH for OUR HEROES served on active duty and recognized that serious needs existed within our military ranks. Many of these needs were not currently being addressed by the U.S. government, or other military charities. There were so many great charities in existence, but the majority of them focused on specific groups or categories: WIA, KIA, bankruptcy, divorce, etc. There were no charities that focused on not only helping military members falling into these extreme categories, but also helping the average, hard-working military member facing a difficult time.

WISH for OUR HEROES understands the impact of military life on not only the military members themselves, but also their families. While one family member is deployed serving their country, the remaining family members are left with a disproportionate workload in 'holding down the fort' back home. Children are severely impacted by the loss of one parent for extended periods of time. A majority of military children under the age of ten have lived without one parent for more than half of their lives! –An astounding statistic.

As mentioned in Chapter 7 of this book, there are several major issues that have plagued our military for quite some time. In Chapter 7, CW3 Dean discussed one of his experiences with the 'Dear John' letter, and also an unfortunate event involving a soldier suicide. For CW3 Dean, these experiences took place during Desert Storm in the early 1990's. Unfortunately, 20 years later, WISH for OUR HEROES continues to deal with these same issues. Not a day goes by that, W4OH doesn't deal with a 'Dear John' letter or a problem resulting from a similar circumstance. The suicide and divorce rates are rising each year in the military, and they are already disproportionately high. Many people don't know that more soldiers died in the U.S. Army in 2010 via suicide than combat. By focusing on assisting military families with smaller issues, W4OH tries to circumvent many of the serious problems facing our military today. Small issues can spiral into larger issues, and larger issues can spiral into things like suicide and divorce. Military life is difficult – men and women selflessly serve our nation, while working for little pay, putting their lives on the line, and dealing with the secondary effects that can tear families apart.

WISH for OUR HEROES is here to face these difficult challenges head-on. Here is how WISH for OUR HEROES works: When a need is identified for a military member (or anyone who knows a military member), the wish (need) is submitted through www.wish4ourheroes.org. A panel of volunteers from W4OH screens each wish and verifies the legitimacy of each request. Once the wish is determined to be a legitimate need, the wish is presented to a 'wish committee', which consists of a rotating board of 3 W4OH board members and 3 volunteers. The 'wish committee' convenes each week (or more often for emergency wishes) to vote and determine the scope and budget granted for each wish. The board of directors for W4OH consists of three Veterans, two of which were wounded in combat.

There are several key facets that set W4OH apart from other charities. One of the biggest is their ratio (administrative and fundraising costs divided by total revenue). The gold standard for charities is to operate at 90 percent, meaning 10 percent goes to administrative and fundraising costs, and the remaining amount goes where funds are truly needed. Most of the better-known charities realistically operate at 70-80 percent, meaning that up to 30 percent of incoming funds are actually distributed to other places (salaries, elaborate events, ad campaigns, etc). W4OH operates at 95 percent, which is unheard of for such a young organization. W4OH has only one paid employee, and is a <u>volunteer-based</u> organization (all other members have normal jobs and volunteer in their spare time). W4OH also strives to provide complete transparency to all donors. For any individual or company who would like to donate, W4OH will work with them to show them all of the wishes currently available, so that the donor can choose which military family they would like to assist.

While W4OH's first priority is to assist military members with basic needs such as food, shelter, transportation, home repairs, clothing, and child needs, occasionally the opportunity arises to develop programs focused on providing fantastic experiences to our troops. W4OH currently has programs in place with the Indianapolis Motor Speedway (more than 30,000 troops sent to races in 2012), the Indiana Pacers, the Indianapolis Colts, the Indianapolis Ice, the Indiana Fever, the San Antonio Spurs, the Houston Rockets, the San Antonio Stock Show & Rodeo, the Texas Motor Speedway, and the Honda Grand

Prix of St. Petersburg, to name a few. While W4OH disburses funds primarily for basic needs (food, shelter, transportation, and child needs), W4OH partners with organizations like those above to receive in kind donations of tickets (and other experiences), then distributes those in-kind donations to our troops.

After only one year in operation, W4OH was thrilled to be accepted into the Combined Federal Campaign (CFC), which is the official list of government supported charities. Today, W4OH is a national 501(c)(3) that grants wishes around the globe. In 2010, W4OH's first full year in operation, they provided $350,000 worth of assistance to our troops. In 2012, W4OH provided more than $2.5 million in assistance! Their largest support bases are in Indiana and Texas, but they have a nationwide team of volunteers. W4OH's ultimate goal is to grant one wish for every deserving member of the U.S. military. To inch closer to their ultimate goal, W4OH partners with both individuals and corporations to enlist volunteers, raise funds, and grant wishes. Types of corporate sponsorships include financial sponsorships, payroll donations (employees given the opportunity to donate a small amount from each paycheck), and wish-granting sponsorships (partnering to grant a specific wish). When working with corporations, there is one rule they always live by: They ensure that any corporation that donates to W4OH will receive a report on the specific military members assisted by those funds. They want each member or employee to understand where their donation went, and what specific military family they assisted.

If you would like to make a donation, learn more about W4OH, or sign up as a volunteer, visit www.wish4ourheroes.org. To stay updated on current wishes, like W4OH on Facebook at www.facebook.com/wishforourheroesinc or follow W4OH on Twitter at @wish4RHeroes.

ABOUT THE AUTHOR

Mike Dean's military career spans three branches (Marines, Navy, and Army) and includes over thirty years of military and civilian service. Mike has an associate degree from Mohegan Community College, a bachelor degree in business from the University of Central Texas, and a master's certificate in government contracting from George Washington University. In addition to a pilot's license, Mike has an FAA airframe and power plant license, is an open water certified scuba diver, and has completed a host of other military schools and special operations training courses.

After serving with Military Intelligence, and being a member of the Unit, Mike retired from the U.S. Army as a chief warrant officer three. His citations and awards include the Bronze Star from Operation Desert Shield/Desert Storm and the Legion of Merit at his retirement. During his career, Mike also taught Principles of Management for Central Texas College in Honduras, owned three small businesses, served as chair of the Consortium for Embedded Systems—National Science Foundation, and graduated from Defense Acquisition University Level Three.

Currently Mike and his wife live in the Midwest, and they are active in their local church and community. Mike is an avid hunter, fisherman, and enjoys riding his Road King Classic.

Mike may be contacted through Wish for Our Heroes Foundation.

ENDNOTES

Prologue

[1] *Killer Elite*, Michael Smith, copyright 2006, 2007, St. Martin's Press, 175 Fifth Avenue, New York, N.Y. 10010, pages 40.

Chapter 1

[2] The Center for Justice and Accountability, http://www.cja.org/ article.
[3] "Bosnia: The Turning Point," Mark Danner, *The New York Review of Books*, February 5, 1998.
[4] Ibid.
[5] *Prosecutor v. Karadzic*, Judgment, ICTY.
[6] *Killer Elite*, Michael Smith, copyright 2006, 2007, St. Martin's Press, 175 Fifth Avenue, New York, N.Y. 10010, pages 187-195.

Chapter 2

[7] The International Tribunal for the Former Yugoslavia, Case No. IT-95-5-1, section titled "The Prosecutor of the Tribunal against Rodavan Karadvic and Ratko Mladic."

[8] Excerpted from a report from The Center for Justice and Accountability.
[9] Motion challenging the legal validity and legitimacy of the International Criminal Tribunal for the Former Yugoslavia, 20 November, 2009.
[10] "Karadzic refuses war crimes pleas," *BBC News report*, 29 August, 2008.
[11] Articles: "French Officer Accused of Collaborating with Milosevic Government," By Francis Dubois and Paul Stuart, 11 December 2001; and Le Nouvel Observateur, Paris 3-9 October 1996, "Should Janvier be Held Accountable for the Events at Srebrenica?" by Jacques Julliard.
[12] Excerpt from an article entitled, "France Denies Officer Who Met With Karadzic Compromised Plans for Arrest," *Washington Post*, 24 April 1998. Also see: "Karadzic Capture Foiled by Secret Talks," *Facts on File World News Digest*, 14 May 1998; "The Hunt for Karadzic," *Time Magazine*, 10 August 1998.

Chapter 3

[13] Tim Wiener, *Blank Check: The Pentagon's Black Budget*, Warner, New York, 1990.
[14] Lenahan, *Crippled Eagle: A Historical Perspective of U.S. Special Operations 1976-1996*, Narwhal Press, Charleston, 1998.

Chapter 4

[15] Quotes transmitted to the author by an Indiana War Memorial Specialist.

Chapter 6

[16] *Encyclopedia Britannica* 11th Edition, 1910, p. 657.
[17] Classic Political Jokes by Comedian Bob Hope, compiled by Daniel Kurtzman.
[18] Dickie, John (2004). *Cosa Nostra: A History of the Sicilian Mafia*. London: Hodder & Stoughton.
[19] Ibid.
[20] Price, Major David H., "The Army Aviation Story Part XI; The Mid-1960's.
[21] "1st Cav Div. (Airmobile)," August 1965, Inside Back Cover; "Over the Beach," April 1966, pg. 18.

Chapter 7

[22] Excerpt from General Patton's speech to the Third Army, 5 June 1944.
[23] From a government documentary "The Fires of Kuwait."
[24] Ecclesiastes 9:18.

Chapter 8

[25] Airport information for MHSC at World Aero Data. Data current as of October 2006. Source: DAFIF. Also available at http://www.informationclearinghouse.info/article23123.htm.
[26] Honduras Guide, Jean-Pierre Panet, copyright 1984, Open Road Publishing, Cold Springs Harbor, New York, pg. 139.

Chapter 9

27 Classic Political Jokes by Comedian Bob Hope, compiled by Daniel Kurtzman.
28 *I Was There*, Bob Hope, published by Bob Hope/Hope Enterprises, Inc., 1994, Burbank, CA, page 27.
29 Article: "Army's New Battlefield Surveillance Brigades Ramping Up," *Defense Daily*, 10 February 2009.

Chapter 10

30 Edward Young (1683-1765), English poet, dramatist. *Night Thoughts*, "The Complaint: Night V" (1742-46).

Epilogue

31 *Sketches of William Wesley Woollen, Thomas Wheeler Woollen, and Levin James Woollen*, Three Brothers, Natives of Maryland and Citizens of Indiana, by Western Biographical Publishing Company, Cincinnati, Ohio, 1896, pg. 243.
32 Ibid.
33 Excerpted from a transcription by Cheryl Zufall Parker, Banta, D.D., *History of Johnson County, Indiana*. Chicago, Illinois, Brant & Fuller, page 676.
34 *The American Heritage Dictionary of the English Language, Third Edition*, copyright 1996 by Houghton Mifflin Company.
35 *Sketches of William Wesley Woollen, Thomas Wheeler Woollen, and Levin James Woollen*, Three Brothers, Natives of Maryland and Citizens of Indiana, by Western Biographical Publishing Company, Cincinnati, Ohio, 1896, pg. 245.

[36] Ibid.

[37] *Representative Men of Indiana* (7th District), Western Biographical Publishing Co., 1886, page 244.

[38] Excerpted from *The Way We Lived in North Carolina*, by Elisabeth A. Fenn, Peter H. Wood, Harry L. Watson, Thomas H. Clayton, Sydney Nathans, Thomas C. Parramore, and Jean B. Anderson, published in association with the Office of Archives and History, North Carolina Department of Cultural Resources, December 2003.

[39] *Representative Men of Indiana* (7th District), Western Biographical Publishing Co., 1886, 243.

[40] From the handwritten notes of William W. Woollen.

[41] Ibid., page 243.